APPLE WATCH SERIES 6

THE ULTIMATE BEGINNER'S MANUAL TO USING THE LATEST APPLE WATCH SERIES 6 EASILY WITH TIPS AND TRICKS

BY

FELIX O. COLLINS

LEGAL NOTICE:

Contents

INTRODUCTION

The Apple Watch Series 6 is part of the latest generation of Apple watches, with an on-display display, the S6 chip, a permanent altimeter, and blood oxygen monitoring function, and priced at $ 399.

The Apple Watch Series 6 was on a rampage in September 2020. It is one of Apple's newest watches on Apple's product line, but it is nearing the middle of its product cycle. Apple usually releases new versions of the Apple Watch in September each year, and there's no reason to say that the new Apple Watch Series 7 will not be released normally this fall.

There are indications that the Apple Watch Series 7 will arrive later this year and have been upgraded several times, but only half a year after the device was launched. This means that for many people, it is still a good time to buy the Apple Watch Series 6, but some customers may now want to wait until the new model is released in the fall.

The Apple Watch Series 6 is Apple's most fully-fledged watch, suitable for users looking for features such as blood oxygen monitoring, ECG, which are always on display with better quality. Users looking for a less expensive option should consider the Apple Watch SE. The Apple Watch SE starts at the US $ 279 and offers many important features of the Apple Watch, such as optical sensor rate sensor and fall detection, but the price is very low, allowing for performance and performance.

On the other hand, if the price is your main consideration and you do not need high-quality health features, then the Apple Watch Series 3 may be more affordable than the $ 399 Apple Watch Series 6, as it offers many key features of the Apple Watch, while the price is only $ 199. . The Apple 3 series needs to be somewhat relaxed because it is an older model, such as a smaller display, an older chipset, and no compass, fall detection, ECG and blood oxygen monitoring.

What's new in watchOS 7

Customize and share your clock face Create a clock face with your favorite issues (even more problems from the same app) and share them via text, email, or online link. See Apple Watch Face Sharing.

Apple Watch sleep tracking with watchOS 7 can help you achieve your sleep goals. Just make a bedtime plan and climb into bed. After waking up, check how long you have been sleeping, and look at sleep patterns for the past two weeks. See Use Apple Watch track sleep.

Countdown Cleaning With watchOS 7, the Apple Watch can detect when you start washing your hands and encourage you to adhere to the time recommended by the Global Health Organization. See Set handwriting on Apple Watch.

Managing watches for family members wearing an Apple Watch can benefit children and adults alike. With watchOS 7, you can set up and manage the Apple Watch for children or another member of the family sharing group. See Set your Apple Watch for your family.

What do you mean ... stick to a word or phrase in another language? Siri can translate multiple languages directly into the Apple Watch. See Use Siri on Apple Watch.

If you are using **Apple Watch to unlock your iPhone** (watchOS 7.4) and cover your nose and mouth, you can use Apple Watch to unlock your iPhone safely using Face ID. See unlocking iPhone with Apple Watch.

Exercise in a new way Open the "Workout" app and start some of the new exercises: dance, strength training, basic training, or cooling. View the results of your workout in the "Fitness" app on your iPhone. See Exercise with the Apple Watch.

Ride freely With watchOS 7, the Apple Watch offers cycling routes including maps showing changes in height, bike paths, and busy roads. See Get directions.

Shortcuts Now, with a single tap, you can use the shortcuts you created on the iPhone, and add a clock face as problems. See Use shortcuts in Apple Watch.

Many ways to protect your hearing the Apple Watch can't alert you to loud noises around you, and it can automatically reduce the high volume played by headphones. See Adjust audio.

The **new watch face** uses the Apple Watch Series 4 and the new face watch later (Memoji, GMT, Count Up, Chronograph Pro, Artist, Typograph, and Stripes) to change things. Add color filters to the face of any "image" dial. Check out the face of the Apple Watch and its functions.

Features of watch series 6

make-up

By design, the shell of the Apple Watch Series 6 looks similar to the Apple Watch Series 5, with an ultra-thin bezel display, 40mm and 44mm in diameter to choose from for a wide range of wrists.

The size of the Apple Watch Series 6 is 10.4 mm. Since the launch of the Apple Watch in 2015, there has been a structure similar to Apple's. The AppleWatch Series 6 can be compatible with previous generations of Apple Watch straps without changing the case.

Apple's 40mm model measures 40mm in height and 34mm in width, while the 44mm model is 44mm in height and 38mm in width. Weight varies from 30.5 grams to 47.1 grams, depending on size and furniture, the Apple Watch stainless steel model is the heaviest.

All Apple Watch Series 6 models have a black ceramic and crystal cover, which resides with multiple heart rate monitors, blood oxygen monitoring, and ECG. Compared to Series 5, the number of LEDs at the bottom doubled. The Apple Watch Series 6 has four LED sets and four photodiodes to support health monitoring activities.

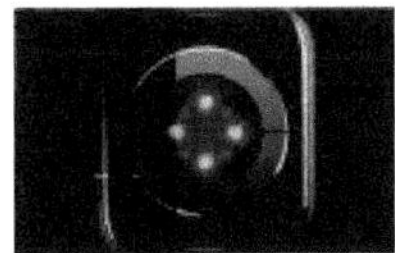

The Digital Crown next to the Apple Watch can be used for navigation purposes, and there is a side button that can be used to call frequently used apps, access emergency services, verify Apple Pay purchases, etc.

Digital Crown is included with the feedback provided to provide a straightforward feel as you scroll through the lists and control the various features of the Apple Watch. This is important for ECG systems because it has a built-in electrode that can be used in conjunction with the Apple Watch. The sensor on Apple Watch.

Please note that the appearance of the Digital Crown differs depending on the Apple Watch model you purchased. LTE models have a red ring around the Digital Crown, so you know they have LTE capabilities, while the GPS-enabled models do not have a red ring.

Frequently displayed

Similar to the Apple Watch Series 5, the Apple Watch Series 6 has OLED ultra-low-power temperature polysilicon and oxide display (LTPO), which keeps the retina display constant, so that time, weight, and other details remain visible without use. When you use the Apple Watch, the screen does not turn black.

With "always open" display, you can see the time without lifting your wrist, and your exercise metrics are always visible when you use the "Workout" app, so you can track metrics like how many calories you burn and how long you stay and how much time you spend.

When the wrist is lowered, the screen will dim to save battery life, but key functions such as the hands of the clock are always on. Touching the dial area or raising the wrist can return the display to full brightness, and to reduce battery usage, Apple has adjusted the dial area for this feature. The Apple Watch display also has a flexible update rate. When the clock is not working, the refresh rate drops from 60Hz down to 1Hz.

When the wrist is low, the permanent display of the Apple Watch Series 6 outside rises 2.5 times, making it easier to see when exercising in the bright sun. There is also a permanent barometric altimeter that can continuously track changes in high altitude hiking, skiing, and other similar activities.

The Apple Watch Series 6 offers many of the same display details as the Apple Watch Series 5, such as the 1000-digit light. The aluminum model Apple Watch uses Ion-X glass to protect the display, while the stainless steel and titanium models use sapphire glass. Crystal Sapphire crystal has better resistance than Ion-X glass because it is more durable, which means that models with sapphire crystal models are resistant to scratches and everyday wear.

The 40mm Apple Watch Series 6 has a resolution of 324 x 394 pixels, while the larger 44mm Apple Watch Series has a resolution of 368 x 448. For the 40mm Apple Watch, this means a display area of 759 square mm, while in a series 47mm Apple Watch is 977mm2 44mm Apple Watch.

No need to force touch again

People with multiple Apple Watch models are familiar with the Force Touch touch, which will appear in menus and settings when you press your finger on the view display. Apple removed Force Touch from watchOS 7, so these actions are no longer available.

You can continue to use all Force Touch-enabled functions with the Apple Watch, but you can use the new swipe action. In most cases, you can use your finger or "digital crown" to scroll down to access other settings to complete all previously performed tasks with a touch of force.

For example, deleting all notifications can be done by swiping down the top notification list. Use the same function to swipe down to write a message in "Messages".

- WatchOS 7 removes Force Touch support from Apple Watch, and that's the only thing that has changed

In some cases, a touch is exchanged with new tones that you can touch, for example, when you right to use controls with the "Camera" app, or you can swipe between new screens (e.g., change the "target" in the "Tasks" Time app. Some options have been moved to the "Settings" app, and in the case of creating a new clock, they have been replaced by longer pressing actions.

Glass Casing

Apple Watch Series 6 uses three materials this year, Apple

canceled the ceramic option and provided aluminum, stainless steel, and Apple Watch alloy models. The aluminum model Apple Watch is the least expensive, while the titanium model is the most expensive.

Apple has introduced two new aluminum colors this year: Royal Blue and PRODUCT RED. Two new colors are options next to traditional silver, space gray, and shades of gold.

Apple Watch's stainless steel versions are available in silver, gold, and graphite colors and are dark gray tones. Titanium varieties are available in natural colors (gray silver) and black.

The Apple Watch aluminum model is made of 100% reusable 7000 series aluminum, lightweight, inexpensive, and designed for active life, while the stainless steel model is heavier, more expensive, and designed for everyday wear rather than sports-focused.

The titanium model Apple Watch has a stainless steel model and a brushed surface treatment, but it is light in weight and easy to clean. Compared to the stainless steel model, the titanium model has a darker and more matte color.

Both stainless steel and titanium have a sapphire crystal display, which is more resistant to scratches than Ion-X aluminum glass. Aluminum models are available with and without LTE connectivity, while stainless steel and titanium models offer LTE only, and there is no cheap GPS model alone.

When it comes to specific weights, the titanium alloy model is 13% lighter than the stainless steel model, the stainless steel model is the heaviest of the Apple Watch models, while some Series 6 models are lighter than the Series 5 models since:

40 mm

- Aluminum: 30.5 grams
- Stainless steel: 39.7 grams
- Titanium: 34.6 g

44 mm

- Aluminum: 36.5 grams
- Stainless steel: 47.1 grams
- Titanium: 41.3 grams

Apple unveiled a special Black Unity Apple Watch 6 series in January with the Black Unity Sports belt. It is an aluminum model of the Apple Watch with an initial price of $ 399. The back of the Apple Watch is engraved with the words "Black Unity", while the rear belt on the belt is engraved with the words "Truth, Power, and Unity".

Water resistance

With the help of signals and grips, Apple Watch models can be immersed in water up to 50 feet deep. The speaker needs air to produce sound and the end of the inlet.

Since the Apple Watch has an average immersion distance of 50m, it can be used while swimming in the water. The sea or swimming pool. However, it is only suitable for shallow-water activities and cannot be used for scuba diving, water skiing, showering, or other activities involving high-speed water or deep penetration.

- How to use the water lock function to drain water from the Apple Watch

The Apple Watch warranty does not cover water damage, so it is best to use caution when dipping the watch into water.

S6 chip

There is a dual-speed S6 System Package (SiP) in the Apple Watch Series 6, based on the A13 Bionic processor used on the iPhone 11.

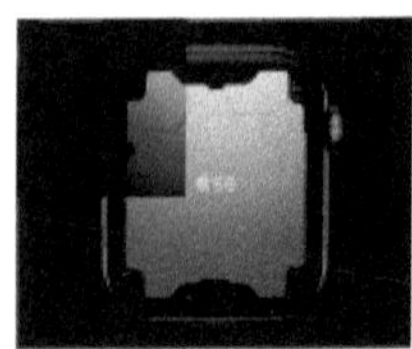

According to Apple, the S6 SiP is 20% faster than the S5 chip of the previous generation Apple Watch, which increases the start-up speed of applications by 20%. It has the same 18-hour battery life, which Apple considers to be a "daily" battery.

Health worker

The Apple 6 series offers the same health functions as Series 5, as well as oxygen monitoring. A second-generation heartbeat sensor can list indicators such as calorie consumption, resting heart rate, and heart rate, while an electronic heartbeat sensor can be used to collect ECG, and new LED and infrared light can detect blood-oxygen monitoring.

A built-in accelerometer and gyroscope can perform other important health-related tasks, such as fall detection.

Apple Watch can detect low heart rate, high heart rate, and abnormal heartbeat, monitor health issues such as atrial fibrillation, and send alerts when abnormalities are detected.

Observing blood oxygen

The Apple Watch rear sensor activates the oxygen-monitoring function found in the Apple Watch Series 6. The oxygen saturation of a healthy person is approximately 95% to 100%. When the oxygen level in the blood falls below this level, it can indicate a serious health problem that needs immediate attention.

Blue, red, and internal LEDs brighten the blood vessels in the wrist, while photodiodes measure the amount of light released from the back. Apple's algorithm then calculates blood color, indicating how much oxygen is present.

Light red blood contains high oxygen content, while black blood contains less oxygen. This is how the Apple Watch determines the oxygen content in the blood. Series 6 can measure oxygen levels in the blood from 70% to 100%.

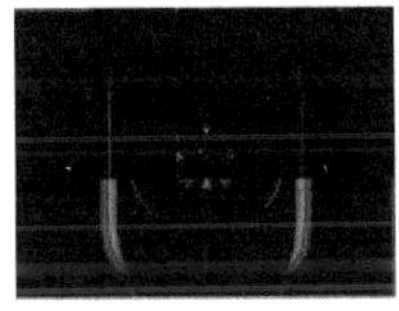

You can use the new Blood Oxygen app installed on your Apple Watch to make blood oxygen levels as required. To measure, make sure the Apple Watch is close to your wrist, open the app, stay still, and keep your wrist flat. Tap the "Start" button, and keep your arm still for 15 seconds.

At the end of the season, Apple Watch will read your blood oxygen level and store data in the iPhone "Health" app.

The Apple Watch Series 6 also did some blood pressure measurements on the back, which was set when the Apple Watch was set up. These settings are existing in the iPhone "Health" app. Browse> Breathing> Spo2> Set SpO2.

The oxygen level is done without exercise, and depending on your daily activities, the amount of reading per day and the time between readings will vary. The effects of oxygen levels in the blood can cause a wick to the wrist to interfere with the darkroom, so if necessary, you can turn off the background measurement of "sleep mode" and "theater mode" with the "Watch" Settings "Apple Watch app.

During sleep, blood oxygen measurement is only done when the "Use Apple Watch sleeps tracking" option is enabled and the clock is used to track sleep.

Staying steady is important for accurate measurements, and the watch should be able to communicate well with the wrist with a strong hand cord. Apple says tattoos affect performance, and skin implants or blood flow to the skin can also affect tattoos. For example, in cold weather, reading may be affected.

Standing such as hanging your arm to your side or placing your fingers in a punch can cause weight loss, exercise can also cause weight loss, and if the heart rate exceeds 150 beats per minute, the Apple Watch will not be able to provide effective blood oxygen reading.

- How to use and diagnose blood oxygen monitoring in

the Apple Watch Series 6

Apple said the oxygen consumption measurement using the Apple Watch Series 6 is not for medical purposes, but for "fitness and health purposes." Since blood oxygen monitoring does not require authorization such as an ECG study, it can be used in more than 100 countries and the list is available on Apple's website.

ECGs

Like the Apple Watch Series 4, the electrodes on the back of the Apple Watch and Digital Crown can work together, allowing users to take one leading ECG. An ECG can measure the electrical activity of the heart and can be used to diagnose health conditions by a physician.

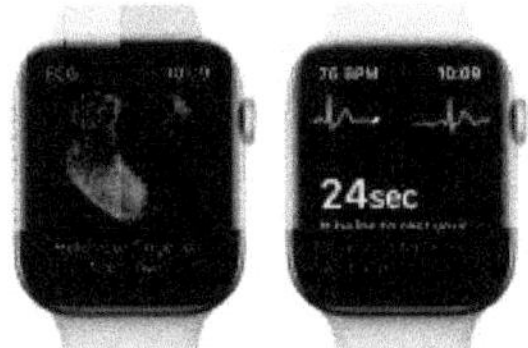

Hold the Apple Watch digital crown with your fingers to capture an ECG, which can detect sinus rhythms (normal), abnormal results, or other uncertain results, and should be shared with your doctor. From watchOS 7.2, an ECG can detect atrial fibrillation at a heart rate of over 100 beats per minute.

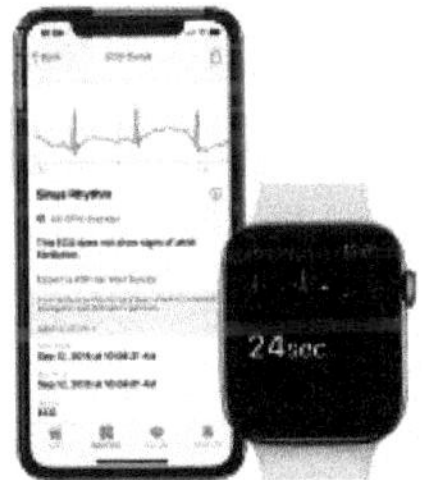

One advanced ECG (such as the Apple Watch) means that there are two areas of communication to measure your electrical energy. A clinical electrocardiogram completed by your doctor may have 6 to 12 guidelines for improving accuracy, but the Apple

Watch offers the opportunity to perform an ECG anytime, anywhere in about 30 seconds.

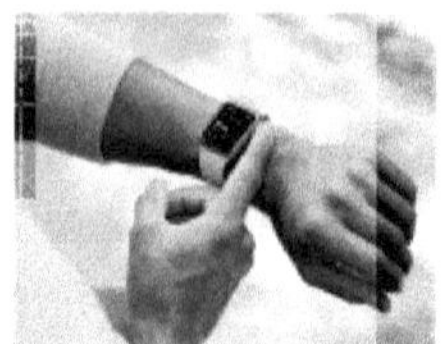

As the ECG feature requires regulatory approval, it is limited to Apple Watch users in certain countries/regions, and the list can be found on Apple's Feature Availability website. Apple has been bringing ECG performance to new countries and has recently introduced it in Australia and Vietnam.

Tracking sleep

With watchOS 7, the Apple Watch Series 6 can be worn at night to monitor your sleep, and Apple can provide data at your bedtime each night. This feature also provides useful tools to bring you better sleep at night. For more information, see our "Sleep Tracking" guide.

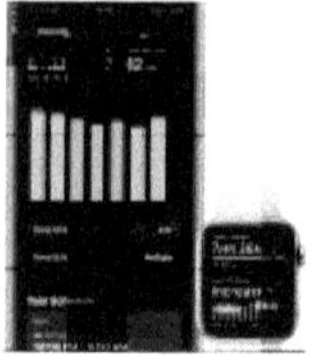

Apple Watch also offers sleep tracking functionality, as it is powered by software rather than hardware, but the Series 6 has better battery performance and faster-charging speed, so you can get the Apple Watch soon after a night's sleep to recharge.

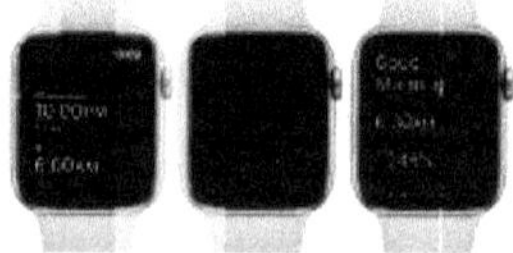

Battery

According to Apple, the Apple Watch Series 6 can offer up to 18 hours of full battery life. The charging speed of the new Apple

Watch is much faster than before, which is useful for features such as "sleep tracking" introduced on watchOS 7.

The 44mm Apple Watch includes a 1.17Wh battery, which is 3.5% larger than the Series 5 battery, while the 40mm Apple Watch includes a 1.024Wh battery, which is 8.5% larger than the Series 5 battery.

The new Apple Watch model can be charged up to 80% per hour or fully charged in 1.5 hours. In Series 5, it takes 2.5 hours to fully charge. Battery life is designed for exercise by tracking internal and external performance.

Apple estimates "daily" battery life based on 90 checks, 90 notifications, 45 minutes of app usage, and 60 minutes of exercise (playing music via Bluetooth). For LTE models, Apple estimates that LTE connectivity will take 4 hours, while the iPhone will take 14 hours.

In some cases, such as when using the phone as a phone or exercising, the Apple Watch uses water immediately. Below are Apple's battery life estimates for each function:

- Play audio from storage for up to 11 hours
- Audio transmission via LTE - up to 8 hours
- LTE talk period up to 1.5 hours
- Home settings battery life up to 14 hours
- Exercise indoors for up to 11 hours
- External Exercise (GPS) - up to 7 hours
- External exercise (GPS + LTE) for up to six hours

Communication

The Apple Watch Series 6 models are fitted with Apple's W3 chip, and there are two variants available: GPS and GPS + Cellular. The GPS + mobile model has a built-in LTE chip and can connect to LTE outside the iPhone, while the GPS model is WiFi-only.

LTE

Since Apple Watch Series 3, an LTE connection has been provided, and with an LTE connection, the Apple Watch is not tied to an iPhone and does not require an iPhone or a well-known WiFi network to connect to the Internet.

However, the Apple Watch is not entirely independent of the iPhone, as LTE communication via an operator requires the Apple Watch and iPhone 6s or later to share a mobile network system with the same user. If there is no iPhone nearby, the Apple Watch does not have a battery that can always be used.

Apple Watch LTE models are available in most countries/regions around the world, and a complete list is available on Apple's website.

U1 chip

Apple added the U1 chip to the Apple Watch Series 6, similar to the Ultra-Wideband chip that launched in the iPhone 11. The U1 chip enables the most accurate wireless cables. Apple said it supports new developments such as the Car Keys, which allows the use of the Apple Watch (or iPhone) instead of the visible car keys.

The U1 chip can also be used to track Apple's upcoming AirTag, which is expected to use U1 technology.

Emergencies

The LTE connection enables the first SOS emergency service released by Series 5. With an SOS emergency, Apple Watch can make calls to international emergency services, regardless of where the device was originally purchased or an active mobile operating system.

This means that if you travel to another country/region with an injury or if you need help, you can activate the SOS function on your Apple Watch by pressing and holding a separate button to automatically contact emergency personnel in that country/ region.

The international emergency call function works in conjunction with the Apple Watch fall detection function. Therefore, if this function is enabled, the clock will automatically send an emergency call when it senses that the user has fallen too far and remains silent.

WiFi, Bluetooth, and GPS

The Apple 5 series supports 5GHz 802.11b / g / n Wi-Fi (higher than Series 5's 2.4GHz) and Bluetooth 5.0. Compared to Bluetooth 4.2, Bluetooth 5.0 offers longer distances, faster speeds, greater streaming message capacity, and better interaction with other wireless technologies.

From Series 2, GPS is integrated into the Apple Watch, and all Serie 6 models (LTE and non-LTE) have a GPS chip that allows the Apple Watch to determine its location without any proximity to the iPhone.

With the help of GPS, Apple Watch can keep track of speed, distance, and route while hiking, jogging, hiking, or cycling to gain a deeper understanding of your fitness activities. GPS, GLONASS, Galileo, and QZSS technology support systems for multiple countries/regions.

Other features

Unlock Face iPhone ID and Apple Watch

We have introduced the "Unlock with Apple Watch" function, which is designed to enable iPhones with Face ID to use an open and authorized Apple Watch as a helpful verification measure when wearing a mask.

Face ID cannot be used when wearing a mask, so the Apple Watch authentication method can prevent iPhone users from always entering passwords while wearing a mask. It's similar to the Apple Watch unlock function on Mac and can be enabled under "Face ID and password" in the "Settings" app.

If you are wearing a mask, an open Apple Watch can be paired with a Face ID to unlock an iPhone, but this is for mask use only. Apple Watch cannot be used to verify ownership of Apple Pay purchases or the App Store, nor can it be used to open applications that require Face ID scanning. In these cases, you need to remove the mask or use a password/password instead.

When the Apple Watch unlocks the iPhone, you will feel a touch on your wrist, and you will receive a notification on the watch, such as how it works when you use the clock to unlock your Mac. Unlocking with Apple Watch is limited to users using iOS 14.5 and watchOS 7.4, and is available for public beta testers and developers. News will be released to the public in the spring.

Sensor

The Apple Watch Series 6 has electronic and optical heartbeat sensors, LEDs, and infrared light to monitor blood oxygen, next-generation accelerometer detectors, gyroscopes, altimeter light sensors -Barometric more efficient to monitor the ascent of stairs, The advantage of height when ascending, etc. Please note that under certain weather conditions, the altimeter may be incorrect.

compass

There is a built-in compass and a Compass app that allows users to view their title, slope, length, height, and current length. The compass function is included in the "Map" app, which allows users to view their gestures when they receive directions.

Storage space

The Apple Watch Series 6 models have 32GB of music and storage space for the program.

No power adapter

The 2020 Apple Watch model does not have a 5W power adapter like previous Apple Watch models. Apple continues to provide Apple Watch ports and charging ports alongside the Apple Watch.

Nike and Hermes brands

The Nike Apple Watch was created in partnership with Nike and is designed specifically for athletes. The Nike Apple Watch models are all made of aluminum, and the price is the same as the standard aluminum of the Apple Watch.

Nike has built special Nike Apple Watch software to encourage runners to stay active. The Nike Apple Watch features a unique Nike design diary, available in silver and black metal, with the same colored straps or Sport Loops, and offers different Nike colors.

The Hermès Apple Watch series is made in partnership with French fashion brand Hermès. Due to the high price of the belt, some of the most expensive Watch Watches offered by Apple have been introduced.

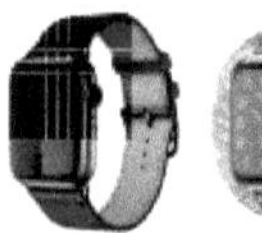  

All Hermès models are fitted with an Apple Watch silver or black metal case, with Hermès handmade leather strap and another Hermes logo for the Apple Watch Sport strap. Hermès Apple Watchs incorporates unique dials based on the design of Hermès watches.

Available bands

Apple built several Apple Watch cables and updated them regularly, introducing new binding options during spring and other news events throughout the year.

Apple offers the Apple Watch Studio feature, which allows multiple strips to be paired with multiple Apple Watch case options, so you no longer need a single Apple Watch thread and case cancellation at the time of purchase.

Available bands include sports belts, sports rings, Milan rings, modern belts, connecting rings, leather connectors, and new single bracelets and single woven bracelets from series 6.

Solo loop

The Sport Loop is similar to the Sport Band but is the first Apple Watch with a faster design and no buckle or fastening device. It is made of a liquid made of stretchy liquid that can be stretched to fit the hand, and then folded so that it fits snugly on the wrist.

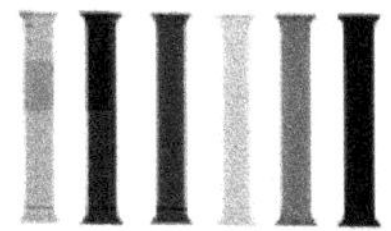

Apple says it is very comfortable because it has no loose parts and is easy to put on and take off. Anti-swimming, anti-sweat, and UV treated with silk effect. The Solo Loop costs $ 49. Unlike all other Apple Watch belt designs, each case size has 9 different sizes.

Apple offers a printable size guide, so you can find a model that fits your wrist, or you can use a tape measure to check the size of your wrist. Because of the large size options, you need to make sure you get the best measurement results before ordering, so please refer to our guide for tips.

Depending on the size requirements, some people have encountered significant problems with the Solo Loop and the Braided Solo Loop, which has resulted in Apple issuing the appropriate instructions. If you use this tool to measure, it should be close but not too tight, and the size between these should be reduced. Apple also warned that the "Solo Loop" will expand over time due to its object. If you need a different size, Apple allows you to come back, but it is better if it fits right away.

Woven Solo Ring

Like the Solo Loop, the Woven Solo Loop is a brand new Apple Watch made without the buckle or clasp type. It is made of a repeating stretch cord attached to silicone thread, so it can be inserted into the hand before being wrapped around the wrist.

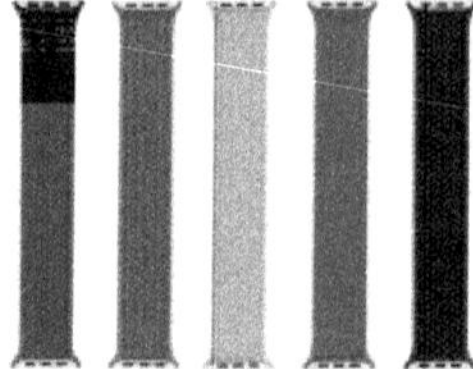

According to Apple, the belt is soft, full of texture, resists sweat and water, and is comfortable to wear. There are 9 Solo Loop sizes woven to the size of each Apple Watch case, so you need to order the wrist size (or stores that sell Apple have the right options).

A solo ring is one of Apple's most expensive band options, costing $ 99, and the same caveat applies to a single bonded ring.

Sports band

Apple's sports hand girdle is a very light and comfortable wrist belt, made of a soft and lightweight fluoroelastomer. Because they are perfect for exercise or hard work, many of Apple's aluminum watches come with Sport Bands.

Sport Bands start at $ 49, which includes three pieces to adjust the size. Apple offers sports hand straps in S / M, M / L, and L / XL

sizes.

Sport Loop

The Sport Loop is designed to be soft, breathable, and lightweight. It is made of fabric wrapped around the wrist, strong and comfortable.

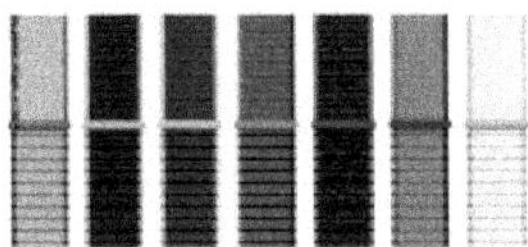

It is made of double-layer nylon such as Velcro, available in a variety of colors, and also offers sporting loops for the Nike brand (Sport Loops). The 40 mm model is suitable for wrists from 130 to 190 mm, while the 44 mm is suitable for wrists from 145 to 220 mm. Apple charges $ 49 per Sport Loop.

Nike Band

The unique Nike Apple Watch belt that comes with Nike watches can be purchased separately.

The Nike belt is made with an effective fluoroelastomer and is suitable for Apple Watch models of 40mm and 44mm. In addition, Apple also sells the Nike brand Sport Loop options with different colors. The hand strap is suitable for wrists with a size of 130 to 200mm. The Nike band costs $ 49.

Milan ring

Milanese Loop of stainless steel is available in two sizes 40mm and 44mm. It is a flexible metal belt wrapped around the wrist. It is made of high-quality metal material, is comfortable to wear all day, and is lightweight.

The Milanese Loop costs $ 99 and comes in silver, gold, and black leather.

Leather ring

The Loop leather, made of Venezuelan leather sewn by Loop, is another belt that wraps the wrist instead of using a bucket. It has two parts, one is fed to the other ring, and then holds itself to get a solid fit. It costs $ 99 and only works on 44mm watches. The leather ring is suitable for wrists of 150mm to 210mm in size.

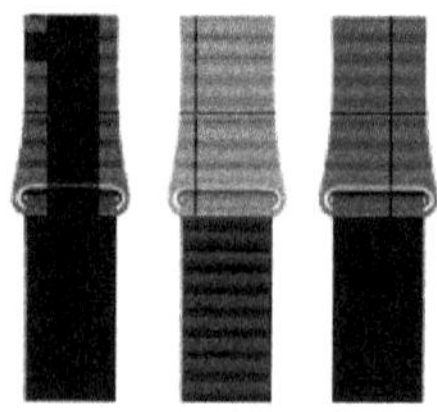

Skin link

Leather Link is a new feature of the Apple Watch Series 6. It is similar to the Leopard Loop, but uses a two-piece design and does not include loops. Leather Link is made of Roux Granada leather imported from France and has a soft magnet that can be tied to the wrist and comfortable to wear.

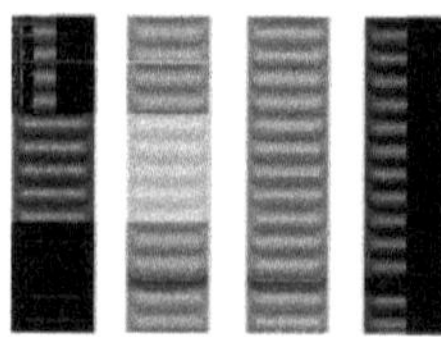

Although the leather ring is not suitable for the small 40mm Apple Watch, the redesigned leather link can be used on both 40mm and 44mm models. Available in medium / small / medium / large size, suitable for wrists from 130 to 180mm in size.

Modern binding

The Modern Buckle belt made of Granada soft leather is designed to work with a small 40mm Apple Watch model. It has two magnetic strips that play a role and the inner layer of the Vectran weave to improve strength and scratch resistance.

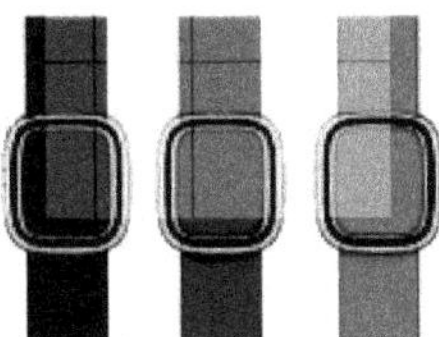

Connect the bracelet

The 316L stainless steel connector bracelet is available in two sizes 40mm and 44mm, and is the most expensive home-made watch by Apple. The Link Bracelet is available in silver (the US $ 349) and black (the US $ 449), similar to high-quality traditional straps.

The 40 mm model is suitable for wrists with a size of 135 to 195 mm, while the 44 mm model is suitable for wrists with a size of 140 to 205 mm. The 6-link add-on kit increases its size from 205mm to 245mm, another $ 49.

Hermes

Apple and Hermès Apple Watch sells a series of independent Hermès cords made by a fashion house. Hermès bands are available in a variety of colors.

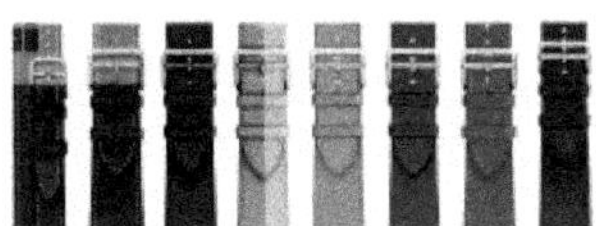

Because these groups were created in partnership with French fashion companies, they are more expensive than Apple's teams.

Hermès teams start at $ 340, then start to rise.

Watchos 7

The Apple Watch Series 6 and Apple Watch SE models use an operating system called watchOS and installed the watchOS 7.

The update for watchOS 7 includes a new face, such as the GMT clock face that shows the most time zones, Counting to find the past, Chronograph Pro with speedometer, Custom Typograph to display numbers, Jeff Artist Jeff McFetridge, Memoji used to put Memoji on Apple Watch also displays lashes with a custom pattern.

The sleep app allows you to track your sleep by wearing your watch at night, providing sleep analysis in an easy-to-understand way. The clock uses an accelerometer to detect subtle breathing-related movements so that it can detect when you are asleep or awake.

The cooling function helps you to establish a healthy sleep mode, and the "sleep mode" automatically turns off the screen and enables "Do not disturb". When you wake up, the Apple Watch will emit a soft sound or use a touch alert and will provide weather reports and battery details to start your day.

WatchOS 7 offers a "family settings" option, iPhone owners can use this option to manage and set up an Apple Watch for children without the iPhone or older family members. Parental control for contacts and downloaded apps, there is a school mode to reduce the performance of the Apple Watch where necessary, and you can use "Find" to track location.

Using family settings, children can call and text their parents, talk to Siri, play music, download apps, use the new Memoji app to create a Memoji, and use Apple Pay with the money given by its parents. Family Sharing includes the “Work Tracking” option, which provides “walking minutes” instead of used work calories, and activity tracking is tailored to children.

There is a very useful handwriting job because we wash our hands more often than usual. It allows the Apple Watch to hear the sound of water and starts a 20 timer to remind you to wash your hands at the right time.

The "Activity" app has been renamed "Fit" and has a complete interface. Later this year, the "Fitness" app could be used with the new "Fitness +" service, which allows Apple Watch owners to use Apple TV, Access Guided to use on iPhone and iPad. The new Fitness app also allows users to customize exercise goals, including standing time and exercise. Apple Watch can measure the minimum distance of VO2 max, the speed of the stairs, the speed of the stairs and the walking distance of six minutes, all of which can be healthy "Available in the app.

Apple has introduced the Apple Fitness + fitness app specifically designed for the Apple Watch, which can be used with an iPhone, iPad, or Apple TV, and provides home fitness services in the Fitness app on these devices. With Apple Fitness +, viewing indicators will be displayed on-screen during exercise, and various tests can be performed. More information about Apple Fitness + can be found in our Fitness + guide.

The Bicycle Route Map app is compatible with the new cycling activity on the iPhone, and Siri now offers voice translation. Apple has also introduced a new Apple Watch Siri shortcut system, so you can access all the shortcuts directly on your wrist.

WatchOS 7 has played a major role in protecting your hearing health by listening to notifications once a week and the option to automatically reduce the volume when installing headphones. Setting the volume up also helps prevent hearing damage

There are many new features in watchOS 7, so be sure to check out our full watch of watchOS 7 for detailed information, as well as some hints for hidden features.

Set up and get started

let's get started

It only takes a few minutes to activate the Apple Watch.

Pair the Apple Watch with the iPhone

To set the Apple Watch, fasten it firmly to your wrist, then press and hold the side button to open it. Put your iPhone next to your watch and follow the instructions on the screen. To set up your family's Apple Watch, tap Set as Family.

Choose a clock face

The Apple Watch comes with many attractive and helpful dials. To switch to another face, swipe left or right on the screen. To see available faces, touch and hold the display, swipe left until you see the "Add" button, tap, and scroll to face. Tap one to use.

Open the app

The Apple Watch comes with a variety of apps that allow you to stay healthy, exercise, and stay connected. To open the app, press Digital Crown, and then tap the app. To come back to the home screen, press the digital crown again. You can download other apps from the App Store on Apple Watch.

Quickly change settings

The control center gives you instant access to silent mode, "do not disturb", Wi-Fi, flashlight, and other functions, such as the iPhone. To open the control center, touch and hold down the screen, then swipe up.

Want to know more? First, set up an Apple Watch and pair it with an iPhone, set up an Apple Watch for family members, select another clock face, open the app on the home screen, and use the control center on the Apple Watch.

Set up and link your Apple Watch with iPhone

To use your Apple Watch Series 3 or later with watchOS 7, you want to pair your Apple Watch with an iPhone 6s or later with iOS 14 or. Setup assistants on your iPhone and Apple Watch work organized to help you link and set up your Apple Watch.

WARNING: To sidestep injury, read Important safety info for Apple Watch before using your Apple Watch.

Turn on, link, and set up your Apple Watch

1. Put your Apple Watch on your wrist. Adjust the band or pick a band size so your Apple Watch fits closely but at ease on your wrist.

For info about changing the band on your Apple Watch, see Remove, change, and clip Apple Watch bands.

2. To turn on your Apple Watch, press and grip the side button until you see the Apple logo.
3. Carry your iPhone near your Apple Watch, wait for the Apple Watch pairing screen to appear on your iPhone, then tap Continue.

Or exposed the Apple Watch app on your iPhone, then tap Pair New Watch.

4. When encouraged, position your iPhone so that your Apple Watch appears in the viewfinder in the Apple Watch app. This pairs the two devices.
5. Tap Set Up for Me. Follow the directives on your iPhone and Apple Watch to finish the setup.

Tip: If you have trouble seeing your Apple Watch or iPhone, VoiceOver or Zoom can help—even during setup while it's linking with your iPhone, your Apple Watch provides tips on how to relate with it. Tap Show, Digital Crown, and Side Button to study more.

You can initiate cellular service on your Apple Watch during setup. If you don't wish to, you can initiate it later in the Apple Watch app on your iPhone. Apple Watch with a cellular network.

Your iPhone and Apple Watch need to use the same cellular carrier. Though, if you set up an Apple Watch for someone in your Family Sharing group, you may use a cellular carrier different from the one used on the iPhone you manage it with.

Cellular service not available in all regions.

Trouble pairing?

- If you see a watch face while you're trying to pair: Your Apple Watch is already paired to an iPhone. You need to first delete all Apple Watch content and reset settings.
- If the camera doesn't start the pairing method: tap Pair Apple Watch Manually at the bottom of the iPhone screen and keep an eye on the onscreen instructions.
- If Apple Watch isn't pairing with iPhone: See the Apple Support article If your Apple Watch isn't linked or paired with your iPhone.

Unpair Apple Watch

1. Exposed the Apple Watch app on your iPhone.
2. Click My Watch, then click All Watches at the top of the screen.
3. Tap the Info button next to the Apple Watch you want to unpair, then tap Unpair Apple Watch.

Pair more than one Apple Watch

You can pair a different Apple Watch in the same way you paired your first one. Move your iPhone near your Apple Watch, wait for the Apple Watch pairing screen to appear on your iPhone, then tap Pair. Or follow these steps:

1. Exposed the Apple Watch app on your iPhone.

2. Click My Watch, then tap All Watches at the bottom of the screen.
3. Click Pair New Watch, then follow the onscreen directives.

To pick up how to set up a watch for someone in your Family Sharing group, see Set up Apple Watch for a family member.

Quickly switch to a different Apple Watch

Your iPhone notices the paired Apple Watch you're wearing and automatically links to it. Just put on a not the same Apple Watch and raise your wrist.

You can also select an Apple Watch manually:

1. Exposed the Apple Watch app on your iPhone.
2. Click My Watch, then click All Watches at the top of the screen.
3. Turn off Auto Switch.

To see if your Apple Watch is linked to your iPhone, touch and hold the bottom of the watch screen, swipe up to open Control Center, then look for the Linked status icon.

In the All Watches screen of the Apple Watch app, a checkmark displays the active Apple Watch.

Pair Apple Watch to a new iPhone

If your Apple Watch is team up to your old iPhone and you currently want to pair it with your new iPhone, follow these steps:

1. Use iCloud Backup to back up the iPhone now paired to your Apple Watch (see the iPhone User Guide for more

info).

2. Set up your new iPhone. On the Apps & Data screen, select to restore from an iCloud backup, then select the latest backup.
3. Carry on the iPhone set up and, when driven, choose to use your Apple Watch with your new iPhone.

When the iPhone operation completes, your Apple Watch prompts you to pair it with the new iPhone. Click OK on your Apple Watch, then enter its passcode.

For more info, see the Apple Care article on How to pair your Apple Watch with a new iPhone.

Transfer an existing cellular blueprint to a new Apple Watch

You can transfer your current cellular plan from your Apple Watch with cellular to another Apple Watch by following these steps:

1. While wearing your Apple Watch, not built up the Apple Watch app on your iPhone.
2. Tap My Watch, tap Cellular, then tap the Info button next to your cellular plan.
3. Click Remove [name of carrier] Plan, then approve your choice.

You may want to contact your carrier to remove this Apple Watch from your cellular plan.

4. Remove your old watch, put on your other Apple Watch with cellular, tap My Watch, then tap Cellular.

Follow the directives to activate your watch for cellular.

For more info about setup and pairing, see the Apple Support article Set up your Apple Watch.

If you want to charge your Apple Watch before setup, see Charge Apple Watch.

Use the Apple Watch to track important health information

The Apple Watch can help you achieve your sleep goals, track significant information related to your heart, monitor blood oxygen levels, and raise your spirits to wash your hands.

Sleep first

The Apple Watch can help you create a sleep schedule, track sleep, and report sleep styles for some time. First, please open the "Health" app on your iPhone and make a sleep plan. Then put the clock on the bed, and the Apple Watch can do everything else.

.

Get a heart health notification

You can enable notifications in the Heart Rate app on your Apple Watch to remind you that your heart rate is too high or too low. If you find an abnormal heart rhythm that triggers atrial fibrillation, an unusual heart rate notification on the Apple Watch will remind you again. Open the Apple Watch app on your iPhone, go to "My Watch", and then tap "Heart". Turn on "High Heart Rate" or "Low Heart Rate", then set a heart rate limit, and turn on unusual rhythm notifications.

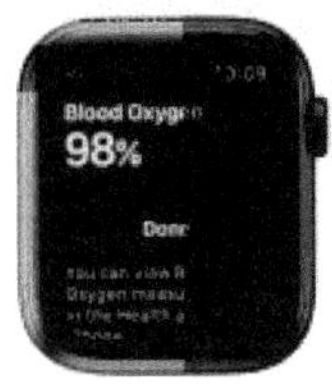

.

Check your oxygen level (with Apple Watch Series 6 only)

Use the "Blood Oxygen" app to measure blood oxygen levels directly from your wrist. View the latest rating results on the Apple Watch, and view the record of all readings in the iPhone Health app.

Wash your hands thoroughly

Turn on the "hand washing" function in the Apple Watch app on your iPhone, and Apple Watch will encourage you to continue for 20 seconds, which is the time recommended by the Global Health Organization. A watch can also alert you if you do not wash your hands within minutes of returning home.

Track your menstrual cycle

Use the "Cycle Tracking" app to record daily details about your menstrual cycle. The app uses this information to provide growth time as well as growth time predictions.

Want to know more? It started with using Apple Watch to track sleep, check your heart rate, use Apple Watch to measure blood oxygen (for Apple Watch Series 6 only), set up handwashing on Apple Watch, and use rotation tracking on Apple Watch.

Lock or unlock Apple Watch

Open the Apple Watch

You can manually unlock the Apple Watch by entering a password, or set it to automatically unlock when you unlock the iPhone.

- Enter password: activate Apple Watch, enter watch password, and click OK.
- To unlock Apple Watch when unlocking iPhone: Open the "Settings" app on Apple Watch, touch "Password", and then turn on "Unlock with iPhone".

You can also open the Apple Watch app on your iPhone, touch "Password", and open "Unlock with iPhone".

Your iPhone must be within the standard Bluetooth range (approximately 33 meters or 10 meters) of the Apple Watch to unlock it. If the Bluetooth function on the Apple Watch is turned off, enter the password on the Apple Watch to unlock it.

Tip: Your Apple Watch passcode may be different than your iPhone passcode, actually using a different passcode.

change Password

You can follow the steps below to change the password created when you set up your Apple Watch for the first time:

1. Not built up the "Settings" app on your Apple Watch.
2. Tap "Password," then tap "Change password," and follow the on-screen instructions.

You can also open the Apple Watch app on your iPhone, tap "My Watch", tap "Password", then tap "Change Password" and follow the instructions on the screen.

Tip: To use a four-digit password, open the "Settings" app on your Apple Watch, click "Password", and turn off "Simple Password".

Lock password

1. Not built up the "Settings" app on your Apple Watch.
2. Click Password, then click Lock Password.

You can also open the Apple Watch app on your iPhone, touch "My View", tap "Password", and then tap "Clear Passcode".

Note: If you disable the passcode, you cannot use Apple Pay in Apple Watch.

Automatic lock

By default, if you do not wear the Apple Watch, it will automatically lock. To change wrist settings, do the following.

1. Not built up the "Settings" app on your Apple Watch.
2. Tap "Password", then open or close "Wire Detection".

Turning off wrist detection will affect the following features of the Apple Watch:

- If you use Apple Pay on your Apple Watch, you will be prompted to enter your password at the double click of a separate button to authorize payment.
- Some metrics for "activity" are not available.
- Heart rate checking and reports are turned off.
- The Apple Watch will no longer automatically lock and unlock.
- Even the Apple Watch SE and the Apple Watch Series 4 and the latest versions will not make emergency calls automatically or have received a major impact.

Handlock

1. Touch and hold at the bottom of the screen, then swipe up to open the control center.
2. Tap the "Lock" button.

Note: To lock the Apple Watch manually, wrist detection must be turned off. (Open the "Settings" app on the Apple Watch, click "Password", and close "Wrist Detection".)

The next time you try to use the Apple Watch, you must enter a password.

You can also lock the screen to avoid accidental tapping during exercise. When using the "Workout" app on the Apple Watch, swipe right and tap "Lock." When you start exercising, Apple Watch will use Water Lock to automatically lock the screen.

If you forget your password

If you forget the password, you must delete the Apple Watch. You can do this in the following ways:

- Uninstall the Apple Watch and iPhone to erase the Apple Watch settings and password, and then pair again.
- Reset your Apple Watch, and pair it with your iPhone all over again.

For more info, see If you forget your Apple Watch keyword.

Erase the Apple Watch after 10 unlock attempts

To protect your information, if your watch is lost or stolen, you can set up your Apple Watch to erase its data after 10 consecutive attempts to unlock it with the wrong password.

1. Not built up the "Settings" app on your Apple Watch.
2. Tap "Password" and open "Clear data".

If your Mac is running macOS 10.12 or later, you can use your Apple Watch to turn on your computer.

Change language and direction in Apple Watch

Select a language or region

1. Not built up the Apple Watch app on your iPhone.
2. Tap "My View", go to "General"> "Language and Region", tap "Customize", then tap "View Language."

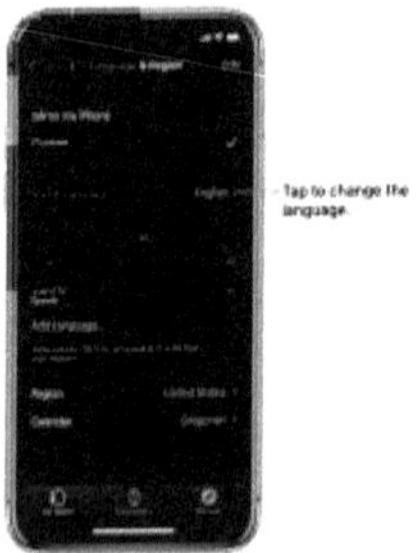

Change the direction of the wrist or the digital crown

If you want to change the Apple Watch to another wrist, or you want to change it to the other side, adjust the steering set to raise your wrist to activate the Apple Watch, and then opening Digital Crown can get things in the direction you want mobile.

1. Not built up the "Settings" app on your Apple Watch
2. Go to General> Direction.

You can also open the Apple Watch app on your iPhone, tap on "My Watch", then go to "General"> "View Directions".

Apple Watch movement

You are using basic gestures to communicate with the Apple Watch.

Tap: Touch a finger on the screen.

Swipe: Change your finger up, down, left, or right on the screen.

Slog: Move your finger through the screen without lifting.

Stay healthy with the Apple Watch

Apple Watch can track your activities and exercise, and encourage you to live a more active life with gentle reminders and friendly games.

Close each ring

The Apple Watch will keep track of how much you move, how much standing, and how much time you exercise each day. Set objectives in the activity app and check your progress throughout the day. Scroll down for more details, such as complete steps and distance. When you complete your goal, Apple Watch will notify you.

Start exercising

Open the "Workout" app and tap the type of exercise you want, such as running, swimming, or dancing. All your statistics will be displayed on a single screen, so you can see your progress at a glance. If you forget to start the workout before the workout, don't worry - Apple Watch recommends that you open the "Workout" app and give credit for the workout you've done.

Use the power of the pedal

With the watchOS 7, the Apple Watch makes it even easier than ever to operate on two wheels by providing you with navigation directions with a map showing altitude changes, bike paths, and busy roads.

How are you

Your latest job statistics look good, but how are they different from last year? A trend can tell you. Not built up the "Fitness" app on your iPhone, click the Summary tab, and swipe up to see activity guide directions to continue or make adjustments.

To learn more about the Apple Watch as an exercise partner, see

Track your daily activities, start exercising, get directions, and watch styles.

Your Apple Watch

This guide grants the Apple Watch Series 3 and exceeding with watchOS 7.4.

Apple Series 6

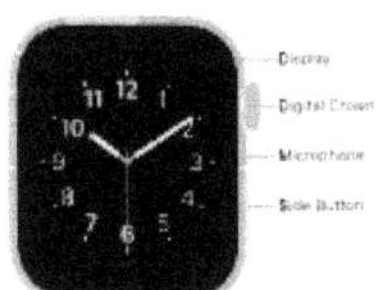

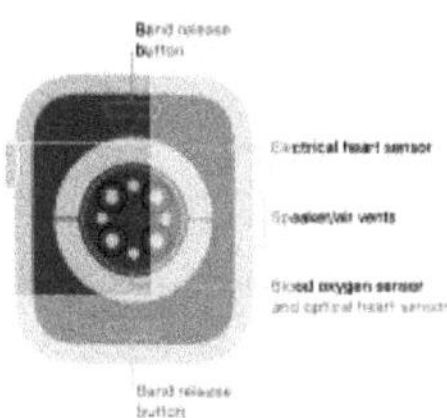

Apple Watch SE

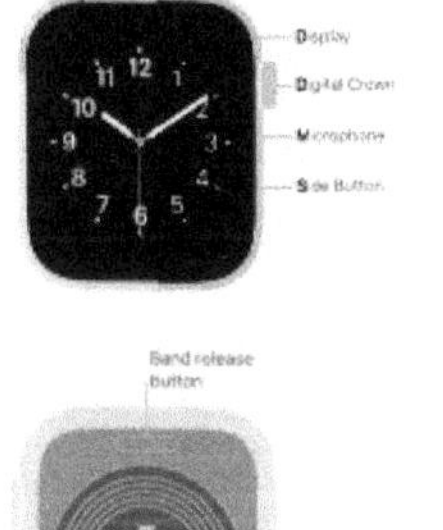

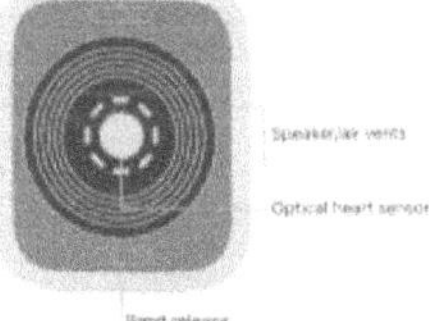

The Apple 4 and Apple Watch Series 5 series

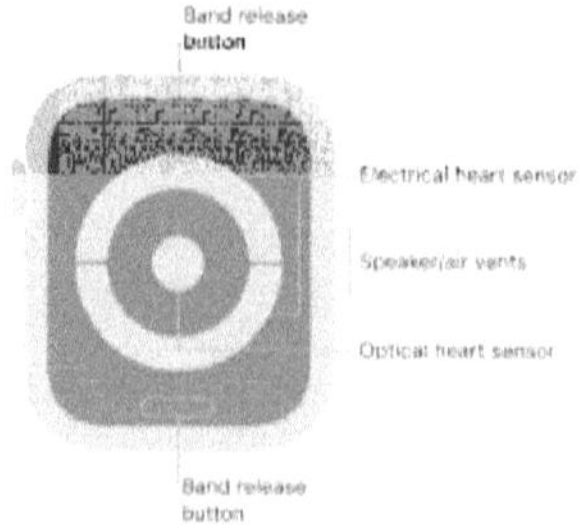

Apple Series 3

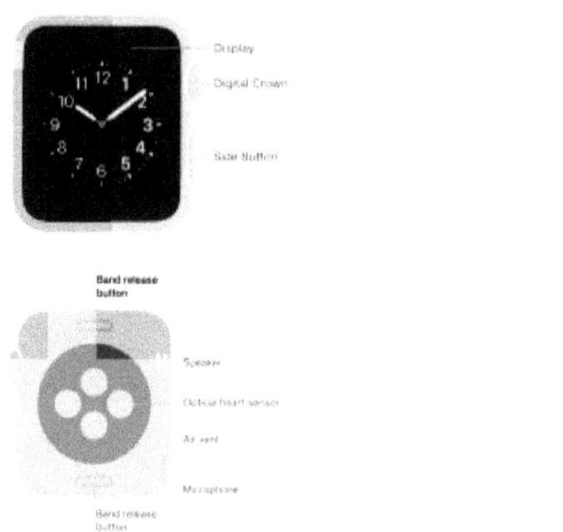

Stay connected to the Apple Watch

Even if your iPhone is not shared with you, the Apple Watch still allows you to easily communicate with friends, family, and colleagues.

Send messages directly from the wrist

Use Siri to respond quickly to messages. When the Apple Watch is linked to Wi-Fi or a mobile network, just raise your wrist and say: Tell mus, I'll not be coming in five minutes." Or touch and grip a message to give your friend a "strike back" "Reply.

Call

Siri can also help you make faster calls. Using an Apple Watch with mobile or Wi-Fi connections, lift your wrist and say "call mom". If you have a Wi-Fi connection, then a simple "FaceTime Mom" can solve the problem.

Announce your arrival

to meet friends? Apple Watch can let them know you've arrived. Not built up the "Find People" app and tap your friend. Scroll up, tap Notification [your friend's name], and choose to notify your friends when they arrive.

Tap and talk

For a quick audio chat, try Walkie-Talkie. Tap your friend's name, touch and hold the call button, then ask "Is it time to chat?"

For more information, see Messaging, Making Calls, Using Apple Watch for Directions or Connecting with Friends, and using Walkie-Talkie.

Charge the Apple Watch

Set the charger

1. In a well-ventilated area, place the Apple Watch good-looking charging cable (included), the MagSafe Duo charger, or the Apple Watch charging base on a flat surface.
2. Connect it to the power adapter (sold separately).
3. Connect the adapter to a power outage.

Start charging the Apple Watch

Place the Apple Watch magnet charging cable behind the Apple Watch. The concave end of the charging cable is magnetically stuck behind the Apple Watch and well-aligned.

When charging starts (unless the Apple Watch is in silent mode), you will hear a tone and see a charging indicator on dialing. When the Apple Watch needs power, the icon is red; when the Apple Watch is charging, the icon is green.

You can charge in a flat area with an open or sloping Apple Watch cable.

- If you are using an Apple Watch magnet charging stand or MagSafe Duo charger: Put your Apple Watch on the base.
- When the battery is low: You can see an image of the Apple Watch's magnetic charging cable and a low battery icon on the screen. For more information, see the Apple Support article If your Apple Watch does not charge or unlock.

Apple Series 6

Apple Watch SE

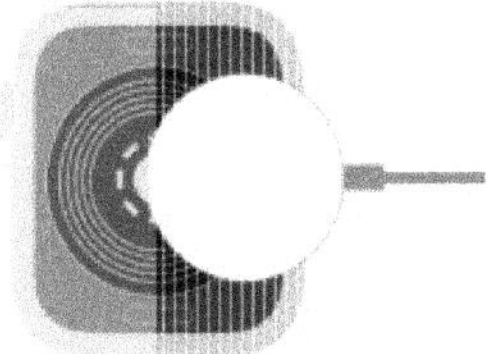

The Apple 4 and Apple Watch Series 5 series

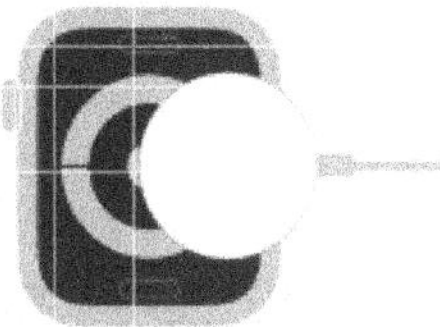

Apple Series 3

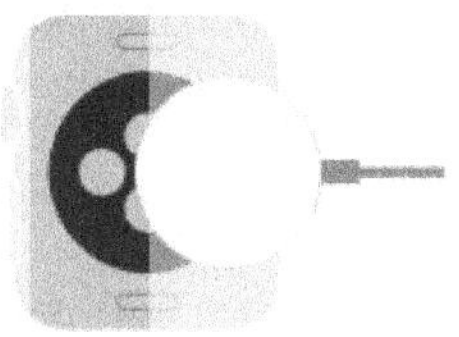

Warning: For important safety information about Apple Watch battery and charging, please refer to Apple Watch Important Safety Information.

Check the remaining battery

To check the remaining battery, tap and hold the bottom of the screen, then swipe up to open the Control Center. To check the remaining power very quickly, add the battery weight to the face of the clock. See the face of the custom clock.

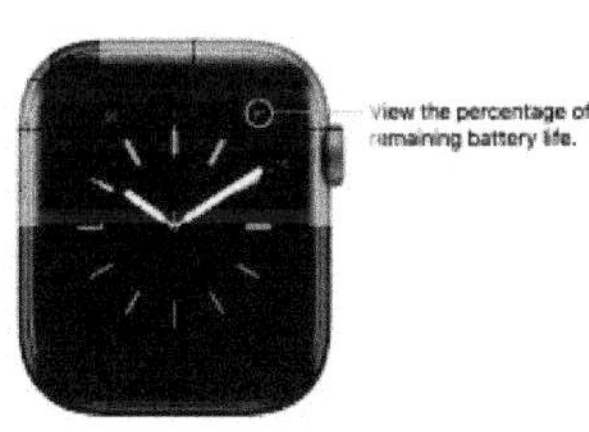

Save energy when the battery is low

You can put your Apple Watch in Power Reserve mode to maximize the remaining battery power. Your Apple Watch is still showing the time, but you can't use the app.

1. Touch and hold at the bottom of the screen, then swipe up to open the control center.
2. Click the battery percentage, then drag the "Power Reserve" slider to the right.

Tip: If you have battery-powered devices (such as AirPods) connected to the Apple Watch via Bluetooth, their remaining power will be displayed on this screen.

When battery power drops to 10% or less, the Apple Watch will crumble inform and allow you to enter Power Reserve mode.

When the Apple Watch almost runs out of power, it will automatically enter Power Reserve mode.

Tip: For tips on extending battery life, see "Extending Battery Life and Life" on Apple's website.

Return to normal power mode

Restart the Apple Watch press and hold the sidebar until the Apple logo appears.

The battery must have at least 10% power to replace the Apple Watch rt.

Check the time from the last charge

1. Not built up the "Settings" app on your Apple Watch.
2. Click on battery.

The battery screen shows the remaining battery percentage, a chart with the latest data on battery charging history, and information about the last battery charging period.

You can also check the time since the iPhone was last charged. Not built up the Apple Watch app on your iPhone, tap My Watch, and go to General> Usage.

Check battery status

You can understand the battery of the Apple Watch battery associated with the new battery.

1. Exposed the Settings app on your Apple Watch.
2. Tap battery, then tap battery life.

If the battery capacity is too low, the Apple Watch will notify you to check service options.

Use enhanced battery charging

To reduce battery aging, Apple Watch uses a machine learning function on your device to read your daily charging process, so it can wait for more than 80% of the charge to be accomplished while waiting for you to use it.

1. Not built up the Settings app on your Apple Watch.
2. Tap battery, then tap battery life.
3. Turn on enhanced battery charging.

Remove, replace and tighten the Apple Watch strap

Please follow the general instructions below to remove, replace and secure the strips.

Make sure you use a thread that matches the size of the Apple Watch case. You can use straps designed for Apple Watch (first generation) or Apple Watch Series 1, 2, and 3 with Apple Watch Series 4, Apple Watch Series 5, Apple Watch SE, and Apple Watch

Series 6, as long as the right size fits. The 38mm and 40mm case straps are equal, while the 42mm and 44mm case straps are equal.

Many straps designed for Apple Watch Series 4, Apple Watch Series 5, Apple Watch SE, and Apple Watch Series 6 can be used with any previous version of the Apple Watch. The Solo Loop and Braided Solo Loop straps are specially designed for Apple Watch Series 4, Apple Watch Series 5, Apple Watch SE also Apple Watch Series 6. Straps designed for the original Apple Watch models can also be used with Apple Watch Series 4 and Apple Watch Series. 5. Apple Watch SE also Apple Watch Series 6.

Remove and change the band

1. Press the band release button on the Apple Watch.
2. Slide the cord to remove it, and slide the new belt into it.

Do not force the band into the structure. If you have trouble removing or installing the wristband, press the wristband release button again.

Fasten your seat belt

For it to work properly, the Apple Watch must fit snugly on the wrist.

For best results, the back of the Apple Watch requires skin contact to detect wrist detection, sensitive information, and heartbeat sensory functions. Wear an Apple Watch well, not too tight, not too loose, and there should be a place where your skin breathes, to stay comfortable and allow the sensor to work properly. In addition, the sensor only works when you wear an Apple Watch on your wrist.

Open and activate the Apple Watch

Turn the Apple Watch on and off

- Turn on: When the Apple Watch is turned off, press and hold the side button until the Apple logo appears (you can see the black screen in a moment).

When the Apple Watch is turned on, a face will appear.

- Turn off: Normally, you always keep your Apple Watch open, but if you need to turn it off, press and hold the sidebar until the slide appears, then drag the "Power Off" slider to the right.

Tip: The Apple Watch cannot be turned off while charging. To turn off the Apple Watch, first, disconnect the charger.

Always going on (Apple Watch Series 5 and Apple Watch Series 6 only)

Always On enables the Apple Watch to display face and dial time, even with the wrist at the bottom. When you lift your wrist, the Apple Watch works perfectly.

1. Not built up the "Settings" app on your Apple Watch.
2. Tap Show and Light, then tap Always.
3. Open is always open.
4. When the wrist is low, open "Hide Sensitive Problems" to hide calendar events, messages, heartbeat, etc.

Turn on the Apple Watch display

You can activate the Apple Watch display in the following ways:

- Raise your wrist. When the wrist is lowered, the Apple Watch will sleep again.
- Tap the indicator or press the number crown.
- Rotate the digital crown at the top.

To do this, open the "Settings" app on your Apple Watch, go to "General"> "Wake Screen", and open "Wake Screen" in Crown Up.

If your Apple Watch doesn't get up when you lift your wrist, make sure you choose the right wrist and stand position. If your Apple Watch does not wake up when you tap on the screen or press or open Digital Crown, it may need to be charged.

Tip: If you do not want to raise your Apple Watch when lifting your wrist, please open the "Settings" app on your Apple Watch, go to "General"> "Wake Screen", and turn off Wake up there your wrist is elevated up. Or, to prevent your Apple Watch from waking up temporarily when you lift your wrist, use theatrical mode.

Back to facial expressions

You can choose the time when the Apple Watch returns to the watch from the open app.

1. Not built up the "Settings" app on your Apple Watch.
2. Go to "General"> "Wake Screen" and make sure the "Wake Wrist Wake" feature is turned on.
3. Scroll down and select where you want the Apple Watch to fall back on: always, after 2 minutes, or after one hour.

You can return to dial by pressing the digital crown.

By default, the settings you select apply to all applications, but you can select a custom time for each application. To do this, tap the app on this screen, tap "Customize", and select setting.

Wake up the last task

In some apps, you can set your Apple Watch to sleep again. These programs include audiobooks, maps, music, current play, podcasts, broadcasts, stopwatches, timers, voice memos, walkie-talkies, and exercise.

1. Not built up the "Settings" app on your Apple Watch.
2. Find General> Raise the screen and make sure the "wrist wrist" function is on.
3. Scroll down and tap the app.
4. Open and return to the application.

To return to the clock face, simply stop your actions in the app, for example, stop a podcast, complete a route on a "map" or cancel the timer.

Keep the Apple Watch display time longer

If you tap to wake up the Apple Watch, you can keep the display longer.

1. Not built up the "Settings" app on your Apple Watch.
2. Go to General> Wake Screen, then click Wake for 70 seconds.

Use the Apple Watch to track important health information

The Apple Watch can help you achieve your sleep goals, track significant information related to your heart, monitor blood oxygen levels, and encourage you to wash your hands.

Sleep first

The Apple Watch can help you create a sleep plan, track sleep, and report sleep patterns for some time. First, please open the

"Health" app on your iPhone and make a sleep plan. Then put the clock on the bed, and the Apple Watch can do everything else.

Get a heart health notification

You can enable notifications in the Heart Rate app on your Apple Watch to remind you that your heart rate is too high or too low. If you find an abnormal heart rhythm that triggers atrial fibrillation, an unusual heart rate notification on the Apple Watch will remind you again. Open the Apple Watch app on your iPhone, go to "My Watch", and then tap "Heart". Turn on "High Heart Rate" or "Low Heart Rate", then set a heart rate limit, and turn on unusual rhythm notifications.

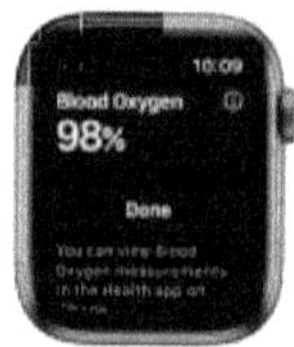

Check your oxygen level (with Apple Watch Series 6)

Use the "Blood Oxygen" app to measure blood oxygen levels directly from your wrist. View the latest rating results on the Apple Watch, and view the record of all readings in the iPhone Health app.

Wash your hands thoroughly

Turn on the "wash hands" function in the Apple Watch app on your iPhone, and Apple Watch will encourage you to continue for 20 seconds, which is the time recommended by the Global Health Organization. A watch can also alert you if you do not wash your hands within minutes of returning home.

Track your menstrual cycle

Use the "Cycle Tracking" app to record daily details about your menstrual cycle. The app uses this information to provide growth time as well as growth time predictions.

Want to know more? It started with using Apple Watch to track sleep, check your heart rate, use Apple Watch to measure blood oxygen (for Apple Watch Series 6 only), set up handwashing on Apple Watch, and use rotation tracking on Apple Watch.

Apple Watch app

Use the Apple Watch app on iPhone to modify the face of the watch, adjust settings and warnings, organize Dock, install apps, and more. For details on finding other apps in the App Store, see Find other apps on Apple Watch.

Open the Apple Watch app

1. On your iPhone, click the Apple Watch app icon.
2. Tap my watch to view Apple Watch settings.

If you pair several Apple Watches with your iPhone, you will see the active Apple Watch settings.

Learn more about the Apple Watch

The "Find out" tab in the Apple Watch app comprehends links to Apple Watch tips, to view all useful information about the Apple Watch, and this user guide, all of which can be viewed on the iPhone.

Apple Watch faces

The face of the Apple Watch and its functions

Your Apple Watch comes with a variety of face clocks, and you can customize most of them. See the face of the custom clock for more details.

See software updates; the following clock face may differ from what you see on your Apple Watch. Not all dials are available in all regions or all models. To check the latest clock, make sure your software is up to date.

Simulation of work

This clock face shows the continuation of your "work" and is elevated to a traditional analog clock. You can choose to view the "active" ring in the standard stack design or as a table below.

- Custom function: color • color (ring or small scale)
- Potential problems: events • alarms • air quality • audiobooks • batteries • blood oxygen (Apple Watch Series 6 only, not available in all regions) • breathing • calendars • camera remote controls • cell phones (cell phones only model) • Compass • Loop Tracking • Date • ECG (not available in all regions or Apple Watch Series 3 or Apple Watch SE) • Altitude (Apple Watch SE and Apple Watch Series 6 only) • Favorites • Find Contacts • Heart Rate • Heart Rate • Home • Email • Map • Message • Monthly • Music • News • Audio • Now Playing • Phone • Podcast • Radio • Rain • Reminder • Remote controller • Shortcut • Sleep • Stock • Stopwatch • Sunrise / Sunset • Time • UV Indicator • Voice Memo • Intercom (not available in all

regions) • Weather • Weather • Wind • Exercise • World Clock

Activity number

This call uses a large and similar font to indicate the time and progress of your "work" in digital format.

- Custom function: colors • seconds
- Potential problems: events • alarms • air quality • audiobooks • batteries • blood oxygen (Apple Watch Series 6 only, not available in all regions) • breathing • calendars • camera remote controls • cell phones (cell phones only model) • Compass • Loop Tracking • Date • ECG (not available in all regions or Apple Watch Series 3 or Apple Watch SE) • Elevation (Apple Watch SE and Apple Watch Series 6 only) • Favorite contacts • Find people • heart rhythm • home • email • map • message • month category • music • news • sound • play • phone • podcast • broadcast • rain • reminder • remote • shortcut • sleep • stock • stopwatch • sunrise/sunset • Time • UV time • Voice memo • Intercom (not available) everywhere) • Weather • Weather • Wind • Exercise • Earth Clock

Artist

Every time you click on the screen, this beautiful face changes in sequence, and there are millions of combinations.

Astronomy

This drive shows the ever-renewed 3D model of the earth, moon, or solar system.

- Custom activity: view (earth, moon, or solar system)
- Potential problems: events • alarms • air quality • audiobooks • batteries • counters • calendars • compasses • dates • altitude (Apple Watch SE and Apple Watch Series 6 only) • heart rate • e-mails • lunar phases • music • news • Audio • Play now • Podcast • Radio • Rain • Aide Memoire • Shortcuts • Stocks • Stopwalks • Sunrise/sunset • Timer • UV indicator • Voice invitations • Weather • Wind • Exercise • Earth clock

Take a deep breath

This dial encourages you to relax and breathe. Just click on the indicator to start.

- Custom functions: style (classic, calm and focused)
- Available issues: events • alarms • air quality • audiobooks • batteries • blood oxygen (Apple Watch Series 6 only, not available in all regions) • breathing • counters • calendars • camera control chemicals • cell phones (phone model mobile-only) • Compass • Loop tracking • Date • ECG (not available in all regions or Apple Watch Series 3 or Apple Watch SE) • Altitude (Apple Watch SE and Apple Watch Series 6 only) • Favorites • Find Contacts • Heart Rate • Heart Rate • Home • Email • Map

• Message • Month • Music • News • Audio • Now Playing • Phone • Podcast • Radio • Rain • Reminder • Remote controller • Shortcut • Sleep • Stock • Stopwatch • Date End / Sunset • Timer • UV Indicator • voice memo • intercom (not available everywhere) • weather • weather • air • exercise • earth clock

California

This call includes Roman and Arabic numbers and is only available on the Apple Watch SE and the Apple Watch Series 4 and above.

- Custom functions: Color • Numbers (pill, Roman, California, Arabic, Arabic, and Sanskrit) • Dial (full screen or circle)
- Potential problems: events • alarms • air quality • audio books • batteries • blood oxygen (Apple Watch Series 6 only and not available in all regions) • breathing • calendars • calculators • camera remote controls • cell phones (Mobile models only) • Compass • Loop tracking • Date • Digital time (full-screen mode) • Earth (full-screen mode) • ECG (not available in all regions or Apple Watch Series 3 or Apple Watch SE) • Altitude (Apple Watch SE and Apple Watch Series 6 only) • Favorite contacts • Find people • Heartbeat • Family • Email • Map • Message • Status (full-screen face) • Month • Music • News • Audio • Now playing • Phone • Podcasts • Radio stations • Rainfall • Remote Reminders • Shortcuts • Sleep • Sun (Full Screen Face) • Solar System (Fixed Screen Face) le) • Stocks • Stopwatches • Sunrise / Sunset • Timings • UV indicators • Voice memo • Intercom (Not available in all regions) • Weather • Weather Weather • Temperature •

Wind • Exercise • Earth Clock

Chronograph

This drive can measure time as accurately as a traditional stop clock. Includes a stopwatch that can be activated directly on the face.

- Custom activity: color • time scale
- Available issues: events • alarms • air quality • audiobooks • batteries • blood oxygen (Apple Watch Series 6 only, not available in all regions) • breathing • counters • calendars • camera control chemicals • cell phones (phone model mobile-only) • Compass • Loop tracking • Date • ECG (not available in all regions or Apple Watch Series 3 or Apple Watch SE) • Altitude (Apple Watch SE and Apple Watch Series 6 only) • Favorites • Find Contacts • Heart Rate • Heart Rate • Home Page • Email • Map • Message • Month • Music • News • Audio • Phone • Podcast • Stream • Rain • Reminder • Remote control • Shortcut • Stock • Sunrise / Sunset • Time • UV Indicator • Voice Memo • Intercom (not available in all regions) • Weather • Weather • Wind • Exercise • Day Clock ba

Timekeeping Pro

Tap the bezel around the primary dial for 12 hours on this drive to convert it to a chronograph. Record time on a scale of 60, 30, 6, or 3 seconds. Or choose a new tachometer time scale to measure speed based on time travel over a set distance. This watch mask is only available on the Apple Watch SE and the Apple Watch Series 4 and above.

- Custom activity: color • time scale
- Available issues: events • alarms • air quality • audiobooks • batteries • blood oxygen (Apple Watch Series 6 only, not available in all regions) • breathing • counters • calendars • camera control chemicals • cell phones (phone model mobile-only) • Compass • Loop tracking • Date • ECG (not available in all regions or Apple Watch Series 3 or Apple Watch SE) • Altitude (Apple Watch SE and Apple Watch Series 6 only) • Favorites • Find Contacts • Heart Rate • Heart Rate • Home • Email • Map • Message • Month • Music • News • Audio • Phone • Podcast • Radio Station • Rain • Reminder • Remote Controller • Shortcut • Sleep • Stock • Sunrise / Sunset • Time • UV Indicator • Voice Memo • Intercom (not available in all regions) • Weather • Weather • Wind • Exercise vocal • World Clock

color

This clock face shows the time and all the activities you add when choosing bright colors.

- Custom Features: Color • Style (circle or dial. Apple-Watch SE and Apple Watch Series 4 and later include full-screen features) • Monogram
- Available problems (circular and flexible styles only): events • alarms • air quality • audiobooks • batteries • blood oxygen (only Apple Watch Series 6, not available

in all regions) • breathing • counters • calendars • Camera remote • Mobile phone (mobile phone) for models only) • Compass • Cycle tracking • Date • ECG (not available in all regions or Apple Watch Series 3 or Apple Watch SE) • Altitude (Only Apple Watch SE and Apple Watch Series 6) • Favorites • Find People • Heart Price • Homepage • Email • Map • Messages • Monogram • Month • Music • News • Audio • Phone • Podcast • Broadcast • Rainwater • Reminder • Shortcut • Shortcut • Sleep • Stocks • Stopwatch • Sunrise / Sunset • Time • Time Indicator • Voice Memo • Intercom (not available in all regions) • Wiseer • Sim o Weather • Wind • Workout • World Clock

Read

Dialing can be used to track the past tense. This watch mask is only available on the Apple Watch SE and the Apple Watch Series 4 and above.

- Custom function: color
- Available problems (circular and flexible styles only): events • alarms • air quality • audiobooks • batteries • blood oxygen (only Apple Watch Series 6, not available in all regions) • breathing • counters • calendars • Camera remote • Mobile phone (mobile phone) for models only) • Compass • Cycle tracking • Date • ECG (not available in all regions or Apple Watch Series 3 or Apple Watch SE) • Altitude (Only Apple Watch SE and Apple Watch Series 6) • Favorites • Find People • Heart Price • Homepage • Email • Map • Messages • Monogram • Month • Music • News • Audio • Phone • Podcast • Broadcast • Rainwater • Reminder • Shortcut • Shortcut • Sleep

• Stocks • Stopwatch • Sunrise / Sunset • Time • Time Indicator • Voice over voice • Intercom (not available in all regions) • Weather u • Weather • Wind • Exercise • Earth clock

To start the timer, tap the primary dial for 12 hours, align the marks on the outer ring in the hand of the minute, open the digital crown to set the time, and tap start. To restore the face to its default state, click the red past button.

Inspector

The Explorer dialing area (with the mobile function on Apple Watch) has a green dot that appears to indicate the power of the mobile signal.

- Custom function: hand color style
- Available issues: events • alarms • air quality • audiobooks • batteries • blood health (Apple Watch Series 6 only, not available in all regions) • breathing • counters • calendars • camera control chemicals • cell phones (mobile phone model only) • Loop tracking • Date • ECG (not available all regions either Apple Watch Series 3 or Apple Watch SE) • Altitude (Apple Watch SE and Apple Watch Series 6 only) • Favorites • Find Contacts • Heart Rate • Heart Rate • Home • Email • Map • Message • Month • Music • News • Now Played • Phone • Podcast • Broadcast • Rain • Reminder • Remote Controller • Shortcut • Sleep • Stock • Stopwatch • Sunrise / Sunset • Time • UV Indicator • Voice memo • Intercom (not provided) for all regions) • Weather • Weather • Wind • Exercise • World Clock

Water and fire

This face clock will heal whenever you lift your wrist or tap the mirror.

- Custom functions: color (fire, water or fire, and water) • style (Apple Watch SE and AppleThe Watch 4 series and above includes full-screen features)
- Available problems (circular only): events • alerts • air quality • audiobooks • batteries • blood oxygen (Apple Watch Series 6 only, not available in all regions) • living • calculator • calendar • camera remote • cell phone (Mobile Model Only) • Compass • Cycle Tracking • Date • ECG (not available in all regions or Apple Watch Series 3 or Apple Watch SE) • Altitude (Apple Watch SE and Apple Watch Series Only 6) • Favorite Contacts • Finding People • Heartbeat • Home • Email • Map • Message • Month • Music • News • Audio • Play Only • Phone • Podcast • Radio • Rain • Reminder • Remote Controller • Shortcut • Shortcut • Sleep • Stocks • Stocks • Stopwatch • Sunrise / Sunset • Time • UV Indicator • Voice Memo • Intercom (not available in all regions) • Weather • Weather • Wind • Exercise Avocal • Earth clock

GMT

This call has two calls: a 12-hour indoor dialing location and 24-hour external dialing that allows you to follow a second-time location. This clock face can be used on Apple Watch SE and Apple Watch Series 4 and above.

- Custom function: color

- Available issues: events • alarms • air quality • audiobooks • batteries • blood oxygen (Apple Watch Series 6 only, not available in all regions) • breathing • counters • calendars • camera control chemicals • cell phones (phone model mobile-only) • Compass • Loop tracking • Date • ECG (not available in all regions or Apple Watch Series 3 or Apple Watch SE) • Altitude (Apple Watch SE and Apple Watch Series 6 only) • Favorites • Find Contacts • Heart Rate • Heart Rate • Home • Email • Map • Message • Month • Music • News • Audio • Phone • Podcast • Radio Station • Rain • Reminder • Remote Controller • Shortcut • Sleep • Stock • Sunrise / Sunset • Time • UV Indicator • Voice Memo • Intercom (not available in all regions) • Weather • Weather • Wind • Exercise vocal • World Clock

To set a second location, tap dial, then open the digital crown to select the time zone. Click the confirmation button to confirm your selection and return to the clock face. The red hand shows you an hour in second place.

Gradient

This watch face is only available on Apple Watch SE and Apple Watch Series 4 and above, and its gradient will change over time.

- Custom functions: color • style • dial (full screen or circle)
- Available issues: events • alarms • air quality • audiobooks • batteries • blood oxygen (Apple Watch Series 6 only, not available in all regions) • breathing • counters • calendars • camera control chemicals • cell phones (phone model mobile-only) • Compass • Loop tracking • Date • ECG (not available on all devices in either Apple

Watch Series 3 or Apple Watch SE) • Altitude (Apple Watch SE and Apple Watch Series 6 only) • Favorites • Find Contacts • Heart Rate • Heart Rate • Home • Email • Map • Message • Month • Music • News • Audio • Phone • Podcast • Broadcast • Rain • Reminder • Remote control • Shortcut • Sleep • Stock • Stopwatch • Sunrise / Sunset • Time • UV Indicator • Memo of voice • Intercom for all regions) • Weather conditions • Weather temperature • Wind • Exercise • Earth clock

Infographics

The clock face has up to eight color-coded and small rich color dials and is only available on the Apple Watch SE and the Apple Watch Series 4 and above.

- Custom function: color
- Available issues: events • alarms • air quality • audiobooks • batteries • blood oxygen (Apple Watch Series 6 only, not available in all regions) • breathing • counters • calendars • camera control chemicals • cell phones (phone model mobile-only) • Compass • Loop tracking • Date • Digital time • Earth • ECG (not available in all regions or Apple Watch Series 3 or Apple Watch SE) • Altitude (Apple Watch SE and Apple Watch Series 6 only) • Favorite contacts • Find items • Heart rate • Home • Email • Map • Message • Monogram • Month • Music • News • Audio • Phone • Podcast • Stream • Rainwater • Reminder • Remote control • Shortcut • Sleep • Solar • Solar system • Stocks • Stopwatch • Sunrise/sunset • Time • UV indicator • Voice memos • Walkie-talkies (not available in all regions) • Climate • Climate temperature • Wind •

Exercise • Earth clock

Modular infographics

The clock face has six rich full-color problems, only available on the Apple Watch SE and the Apple Watch Series 4 and above.

- Custom function: color
- Available problems: functions • air quality • alerts • audiobooks • batteries • blood oxygen (Apple Watch Series 6 only, not available in all regions) • breathing • calculator • calendar • camera remote control • mobile phone (mobile phone model) only) • Compass • Loop tracking • Date • Earth • ECG (not available in all regions or Apple Watch Series 3 or Apple Watch SE) • Altitude (Apple Watch SE and Apple Watch Series 6 Only) • Favorite Contacts • Find People • Heart Rate • Home • Email • Map • Message • Month • Music • News • Audio • Play Only • Phone • Podcast • Stream • Rain • Reminder • Remote control • Shortcut • Shortcut • Sleep • Solar • Solar System • Stock • Stopwatch • Time • UV Indicator • Voice Memo • Intercom-Intercom • Weather • Weather • Wind • Exercise • Earth Clock

kaleidoscope

Choose an image to create a clock face with a variety of shapes and color patterns. Change the digital crown to change the pattern.

- Custom Function: Image • Style (Apple Watch SE and

Apple Watch Series 4 and later includes full-screen feature)

- Available Issues (Facet, Radial and Rosette Styles): Events • Alerts • Air Quality • Audiobooks • Batteries • Spo2 (Apple Watch Series 6 only, not available in all regions) • Breathing • Calculator • Calendar • Camera remote • Phone (for mobile models only) • Compass • Cycle tracking • Day • ECG (not accessible in all counties or Apple Watch Series 3 or Apple Watch SE) • Altitude (Only Apple Watch SE and Apple Watch Series 6) • Favorites • Find People • Heartbeat • Home • Email • Map • Message • Month • Music • News • Audio • Play only • Phone • Podcast • Radio • Rain • Reminder • Shortcut • Shortcut • Shortcut • Sleep • Stocks • Stopwatch • Sunrise / Sunset • Time • UV Indicator • Voice Memo • Intercom (not available in all regions) • Weather • Weather • Winda • Exercise • World clock

Liquid metal

This face clock will heal whenever you lift your wrist or tap the mirror.

- Custom Features: Color • Face (Apple Watch SE and Apple Watch Series 4 and later includes full features)
- Available problems (circular only): events • alerts • air quality • audiobooks • batteries • blood oxygen (Apple Watch Series 6 only, not available in all regions) • breathing • calculator • calendar • camera remote • Mobile phone (Mobile Model Only) • Compass • Cycle Tracking • Date • ECG (not accessible in all counties or Apple Watch Series 3 or Apple Watch SE) • Altitude (Apple Watch SE and Apple Watch Series Only 6) • Favorite Contacts • Finding People • Heartbeat • Home •

Email • Map • Message • Month • Music • News • Audio • Play Only • Phone • Podcast • Radio • Rain • Reminder • Remote Controller • Shortcut • Shortcut • Sleep • Stocks • Stocks • Stopwatch • Sunrise / Sunset • Time • UV Indicator • Voice Memo • Intercom (not available in all regions) • Weather • Weather • Wind • Exercise Avoca • Earth clock

Memoji

This place has a Memoji you created with all the Memoji characters. This watch mask is only available on the Apple Watch SE and the Apple Watch Series 4 and above.

- Custom functions: characters
- Potential problems: events • alarm • air quality • audiobooks • battery • calendar • compass • date • altitude (Apple Watch SE and Apple Watch Series 6 only) • heartbeat • message • music • news • sound • play • Podcasting • Broadcast • Rain • Reminder • Shortcut • Sleep • Stock • Stopwatch • Time • UV Indicator • Wind • Exercise • Earth Clock

meridian

Full-screen dialing is only available on the Apple Watch SE and the Apple Watch Series 4 and above and looks like the creation of four small dials.

- Custom function: color • brush (black or white)
- Problems available: events • alarms • air quality • audio-

books • batteries • blood oxygen (Apple Watch Series 6 only, not available in all regions) • breathing • calendars • calculators • camera remote controls • cell phones (mobile model only) • Compass • Loop tracking • Date • Digital time • Global • ECG (not available in all regions or Apple Watch Series 3 or Apple Watch SE) • Altitude (Apple Watch SE and Apple Watch Series 6) • Favorite Contacts • Finding People • Heart Rate • Home • Email • Map • Message • Monogram • Monthly • Music • News • Audio • Phone • Podcast • Stream • Rainwater • Reminder • Shortcut • Shortcut • Sleep • Solar • Solar System • Stock • Stopwatch • Time> UV Index • Voice over voice • Intercom (not available in all regions) • Weather • Temperature weather • Air • Exercise • Earth clock

Mickey Mouse and Minnie Mouse

Let Mickey Mouse or Minnie Mouse give you an idea of the time — their arms rotate to show the hours and minutes, and their feet beat every second.

- Custom function: color letter •
- Available problems: events • alarms • air quality • audiobooks • batteries • blood oxygen (Apple Watch Series 6 only, not available in all regions) • breathing • counters • calendars • camera control chemicals • cell phones (phone model mobile-only) • Compass • Loop tracking • Date • ECG (not available in all regions or Apple Watch Series 3 or Apple Watch SE) • Altitude (Apple Watch SE and Apple Watch Series Only 6) • Favorites • Find Contacts • Heart Rate • Heart Rate • Home • Email • Map • Message • Monthly • Music • News • Audio • Now Playing • Phone • Podcast • Radio • Rain • Reminder • Shortcut •

Sleep • Stock • Stopwatch • Date Uonly / sunset • timer • UV indicator • voice memo • intercom (not available everywhere) • weather • weather • wind • exercise • world clock

To hear Mickey Mouse or Minnie Mouse telling you the time, open the "Settings" app on your Apple Watch, tap "Clock", and then open "Talk Time". Lift your wrist and put two fingers in the drive to listen for the time.

Modular

This face clock has a digital time indicator and grid layout that allows you to add multiple functions to get the perfect picture of your day.

- Custom function: color
- Potential problems: events • warnings • air quality • audiobooks • batteries • blood oxygen (Apple Watch Series 6 only, not available in all regions) • living • calculator • calendar • camera remote switch • cell phone (cell phone) -dels only) • Compass • Cycle tracking • Date • ECG (not available in all regions or Apple Watch Series 3 or Apple Watch SE) • Altitude (Apple Watch SE and Apple Watch Series 6 only) • Favorite contacts • Search people • Heart rate • Home • Email • Maps • Info • Monthly • Music • News • Audio • Now playing • Calls • Podcasts • Stream • Rain • Reminders • Remote control • Shortcuts • Sleep • Stocks • Sunset stops • Sunrise/sunset • Timings • UV indicators • Voice invitations • Walkie-talkies (not available everywhere) • Status weather • Weather conditions

Modular and compact

With this clock face, which is only available on Apple Watch SE and Apple Watch Series 4 and later, you can choose up to three problems with a digital or analog clock face.

- Custom function: color • dial (analog or digital)
- Potential problems: events • alarms • air quality • audiobooks • batteries • blood oxygen (Apple Watch Series 6 only, not available in all regions) • breathing • counters • calendars • Camera remote controls • cell phones (models mobile-only) • Compass • Loop Tracking • Date • Earth • ECG (not available in all regions or Apple Watch Series 3 or Apple Watch SE) • Altitude (Apple Watch SE and (Apple Watch Series 6) Remote control • Shortcut • Sleep • Solar • Solar system • Stocks • Stopwatch • Times • UV indicator • Voice memos • Walkie-talkies-walkie-talkies (not available in all regions) • Weather • Weather weather • Status of • Exercise • World clock

movement

This clock face shows beautifully animated themes.

- Custom function: choose animated butterflies, flowers, or jellyfish
- Potential problems: events • alarms • air quality • audiobooks • batteries • counters • calendars • compasses • dates • height (Apple Watch SE and Apple Watch Series 6 only) • heart rate • letters • lunar stages • music • news • Audio • Play now • Podcast • Radio • Rain • Aide Memoire • Shortcuts • Stocks • Stopwalks • Sunrise/sunset • Timer

• UV indicator • Voice invitations • Weather • Wind • Exercise • Earth clock

number

This dial indicates the time on the large hand signals. You can choose from seven different fonts and countless colors to achieve the perfect combination.

- Custom function: color • symbol
- Potential problems: events • alarms • air quality • audiobooks • batteries • blood oxygen (Apple Watch Series 6 only, not available in all regions) • unbreathing • counters • calendars • Camera remote controls • cell phones (mobile models only) • Compass • Loop tracking • Date • ECG (not available in all regions or Apple Watch Series 3 or Apple Watch SE) • Altitude (Apple Watch SE and Apple Watch Series 6 only) • Favorite Contacts • Find People • Heart Rate • Family • Email • Map • Message • Month • Music • News • Audio • Phone • Podcast • Radio • Rain • Reminder • Remote control • Shortcut • Sleep • Stock • Stopwatch • Sunrise / Sunset • Time • UV indicator • Voice Memo • Intercom (not available in all regions) • Weather • Weather • Wind • Exercise • World Clock

Digital Duo

This call is especially displayed on the Apple Watch in a font designed for Apple to display a large number of numbers.

- Custom functions: colors • symbols (Arabic, Arabic, Indian, Sanskrit) • styles (fill, mix, outline)

Digital mono

Dialing is especially displayed for the Apple Watch in a font designed for Apple to display a large number of numbers.

- Custom function: color • symbol (Arabic, Arabic, Sanskrit, Roman) • style (fill or outline)

picture

This clock face lets you display photos from the "Photos" app on the Apple Watch. For more photos, please add more than one photo.

- Custom functions: color filters • content (synced albums, favorites, photos, editing capabilities)
- Available issues: Events • Alerts • Air quality • Audiobooks • Batteries • Calculators • Calendars • Compass • Date • Elevation (Only Apple Watch SE and Apple Watch Series 6) • Heart rate • Messages • Month • Music • News • Sound • Play Now • Podcast • Radio • Rain • Reminders • Shortcuts • Stocks • Stopwatchs • Sunrise/sunset • Timer • UV indicator • Weather • Weather • Exercise • Exercise

Each time you lift your wrist or tap t, a new image will appear. He showed up. Choose an album, an internal memory, or up to 24 custom photos.

Create a photo face on Apple Watch: While the current face is displayed, touch and hold the display, swipe right, tap the "New" (+) button, and then tap "Photo". Or, when you browse in the Apple Watch "Photos" app, click the "Face View" button, then click on "Photos".

Create a photo on the iPhone: Open the "Photos" app on the iPhone, click the image, click the "Share" button, swipe up, and then click "Create Face View". Choose to create a face dialing face or a kaleidoscope dialing face.

Install a color filter: On the Apple Watch, touch and hold the "Photo" face, tap "Edit", then turn on Digital Crown to select a color filter. On the iPhone, open the Apple Watch app, go to "Face Gallery"> "Photos", and select a color filter.

If you do not see the photos, please make sure they are in your synced album. For help, see Select album and manage storage in Apple Watch.

Analog Pride

This face is inspired by the rainbow flag. When you tap the face or open the digital crown, the colored lines will go.

- Custom function: style (Apple Watch SE and Apple Watch Series 4 and later include full-screen feature)
- Available issues (circular pattern problems only): Events • Alerts • Air quality • Audiobooks • Batteries • Spo2 (Apple Watch Series 6 only and not available in all regions) • Respiration • Calculator • Calendar • Camera controller remote • Mobile phone) for models only) • Compass • Cycle track • Date • ECG (not available in all regions or Apple Watch Series 3 or Apple Watch SE) • Altitude (Apple Watch SE only and Apple Watch Series

6) • Favorites • Find people • Heart rate • Family • Email • Map • Information • Month • Music • News • Audio • Phone •Podcast • Broadcast • Rain • Reminder • Remote control • Shortcut button • Sleep • Stocks • Stopwatch • Sunrise / Sunset • Time • UV Time • Voice over • Intercom (not available in all regions) • Weather • Weather • Wind • Exercise • Earth clock

Tip: You can add a "Proud" look to many other face faces. Not built up the Apple Watch app on your iPhone, tap Face Gallery, and under Superiority, choose the many California color options, Figures Duo, Numbers Mono, and Gradient dials.

Pride Digital

This face is inspired by the rainbow flag. When you tap the face or open the digital crown, the colored lines will go.

- Custom work: style (2018 or 2019)
- Potential problems: events • alarms • air quality • audiobooks • batteries • counters • calendars • compasses • dates • altitude (Apple Watch SE and Apple Watch Series 6 only) • heart rate • memos • lunar phases • music • news • Audio • Play now • Podcast • Radio • Rain • Aide Memoire • Shortcuts • Stocks • Stopwalks • Sunrise/sunset • Timer • UV indicator • Voice invitations • Weather • Wind • Exercise • Earth clock

Tip: You can add a "Proud" look to many other faces. Exposed the Apple Watch app on your iPhone, tap Face Gallery, and under Superiority, select the many California color options, Figures Duo, Numerals Mono, and Gradient dials.

Simple

This simple and elegant dial allows you to add details to the drive and add functions to the corners.

- Custom function: color style
- Possible problems: events • alarms • air quality • audiobooks • batteries • blood oxygen (Apple Watch Series 6 only, not available in all regions) • breathing • counters • calendars • Camera remote controls • cell phones (models mobile-only) • Compass • Loop tracking • Date • ECG (not available in all regions or Apple Watch Series 3 or Apple Watch SE) • Altitude (Apple Watch SE and Apple Watch Series 6 only) • Favorite Contacts • Find People • Heart Rate • Family • Email • Map • Message • Month • Music • News • Audio • Phone • Podcast • Radio • Rain • Reminder • Remote control • Shortcut • Sleep • Stock • Stopwatch • Sunrise / Sunset • Time • UV indicator • Voice Memo • Intercom (not available in all regions) • Weather • Weather • Wind • Exercise • Earth Clock

Siri

Siri will use this face to view your day and show timely and helpful details. This could be your next appointment, home traffic, or sunset time, you can click to get more details. You can also change Digital Crown to scroll all day.

- Custom function: color
- Available issues: events • alerts • air quality • audio-

books • batteries • blood oxygen (only Apple Watch Series 6, not available in all regions) • breathing • calculator • calendar • mobile phone (mobile phone model only) • compass • Round Tracking • Date • ECG (not available in all constituencies or Apple Watch Series 3 or Apple Watch SE) • Altitude (Only Apple Watch SE and Apple Watch Series 6) • Regular Contacts • Find People • Heart Rate • Heart • Home • Email • Map • Message • Month • Music • News • Audio • Phone • Podcast • Broadcast • Rain • Reminder • Remote control • Siri • Stock • Stopwatch • Sunrise / Sunset • Time • UV Index • Voice Memo • Walkie-talkie (not available in all regions) • weather • weather • wind • exercise • world clock

The sun

Depending on your current location and time of day, Solar dialing will show the location of the Sun in the sky as well as the date, day, and current time.

- Potential problems: events • alarms • air quality • audiobooks • batteries • counters • calendars • computer computers • compass • dates • altitude (Apple Watch SE and Apple Watch Series 6 only) • heart rhythm • messages • months Section • Music • News • Audio • Play Now • Podcast • Broadcast • Rain • Reminder • Shortcut • Sleep • Stock • Stopwatch • Sunrise / Sunset • Time • UV Indicator • Voice Memo • Weather • Wind • Exercise • World clock

Dialing in the sun

This dial surface (available on Apple Watch SE and Apple Watch Series 4 and later) has a 24-hour orientation that can track the sun, as well as an analog or digital dial opposite the solar system.

Tip: Tap the clock to view the time of day.

- Custom function: call (analog or digital)
- Available issues: events • alerts • air quality • audiobooks • battery • blood oxygen (only Apple Watch Series 6, not available in all regions) • breathing • calculator • calendar • mobile phone (mobile phone model only) • compass • Loop tracking • Date • ECG (not available in all regions or Apple Watch Series 3 or Apple Watch SE) • Elevation (Apple Watch SE and Apple Watch Series 6 only) • Frequent contacts • Find people • Heartbeat • Heart • Home • Email • Map • Message • Month • Music • News • Audio • Phone • Podcast • Broadcast • Rain • Reminder • Remote control • Stock • Stopwatch • Sunrise / Sunset • Time • UV Indicator • Voice Invitation • Walkie - talkie (not available in all regions) • weather conditions • tropical heat • wind • exercise • world clock

Line

In this brush, you can select the number of strokes you want, select a color and rotate the angle. This watch mask is only available on the Apple Watch SE and the Apple Watch Series 4 and above.

- Custom functions: style • number of strokes • color of stripes
- Available issues (problems only in a circular pattern):

Events • Alerts • Air quality • Audiobooks • Batteries • Spo2 (Apple Watch Series 6 only and not available in all regions) • Respiration • Calculator • Calendar • Camera Remote control • Mobile (mobile) for models only) • Compass • Cycle tracking • Date • ECG (not available in all regions or Apple Watch Series 3 or Apple Watch SE) • Altitude (Apple Watch SE only with Apple Watch Series 6) • Favorites Find People • Heart Price • Family • Email • Map • Info • Month • Music • News • Audio • Phone • Podcast • Stream • Rain • Reminder • Sleep Key • Sleep • Stocks • Stopwatch • Sunrise / Sunset • Time • UV indicator • Voice Memo • Intercom (not available in all regions) • Weather • Wind • Exercise • Earth clock

Time is running out

The clock face shows a timeless video of a natural scene or city location of your choice.

- Custom activity: select a video of Mack Lake, New York, Hong Kong, London, Paris, or Shanghai
- Available issues: Events • Alerts • Air quality • Audiobooks • Battery • Calculator • Calendar • Compass • Day • Elevation (Apple Watch SE and Apple Watch Series 6 only) • Heart rate • Message • Month • Music • News • Audio • Now Playable • Podcast • Radio • Rain • Reminder • Stock • Stopwatch • Sunrise / Sunset • Time • UV Indicator • Voice Memo • Weather • Weather • Exercise • Earth Clock

Toy Story

Your favorite toy character lives by using a rai wrist.

- Custom activity: character (select "Toy Box", "Buzz", "Woody" or "Jesse")
- Potential problems: events • alarms • air quality • audiobooks • batteries • counters • calendars • compasses • dates • altitude (Apple Watch SE and Apple Watch Series 6 only) • heart rate • memos • lunar phases • music • news • Audio • Play now • Podcast • Radio • Rain • Reminders • Shortcuts • Stocks • Stopwalks • Sunrise/sunset • Timer • UV indicator • Voice invitations • Weather • Wind • Exercise • Earth clock

Typograph

This call has three custom fonts. This watch mask is only available on the Apple Watch SE and the Apple Watch Series 4 and above.

- Custom functions: color • style • font • script
- Available issues: date • digital time • monogram • stopwatch • timer

Unity

These drives are available in Apple Watch SE and Apple Watch Series 4 and other latest versions of watchOS 7.3 and beyond, and are promoted in Pan-African flag colors. The mood will change as you move to create your unique face.

- Custom function: color
- Potential problems: events • warnings • air quality • audiobooks • battery • calendar • compass • date • height • heart rate • message • monthly phase • music • news • play now • podcast • radio • rain • Reminder • Stock • Stopwatch • Sunrise / Sunset • Time • UV indicator • Weather • Weather • Wind • Exercise • Earth clock

Utility

This drive is active and efficient. You can add up to three problems to show what you want to see at a glance.

- Custom function: color style •
- Available issues: events • alarms • air quality • audiobooks • batteries • blood oxygen (Apple Watch Series 6 only, not available in all regions) • breathing • counters • calendars • camera control chemicals • cell phones (phone model mobile-only) • Compass • Loop tracking • Date • ECG (not available in all regions or Apple Watch Series 3 or Apple Watch SE) • Altitude (Apple Watch SE and Apple Watch Series 6 only) • Favorites • Find Contacts • Heart Rate • Heart Rate • Home • Email • Map • Message • Month • Music • News • Audio • Now Playing • Phone • Podcast • Radio • Rain • Reminder • Remote controller • Shortcut • Sleep • Stock • Stopwatch • Date End / Sunset • Timer • UV Indicator • voice memo • intercom (not available everywhere) • weather • weather • air • ex-

ercise • earth clock

Vapor

This face clock will heal whenever you lift your wrist or tap the mirror.

- Custom features: • color style (Apple Watch SE and Apple Watch Series 4 and later includes full-screen features)
- Available problems (circular only): events • alerts • air quality • audiobooks • batteries • blood oxygen (Apple Watch Series 6 only, not available in all regions) • breathing • adding machine • datebook • camera remote • Mobile phone (Mobile Model Only) • Compass • Cycle Tracking • Date • ECG (not available in all regions or Apple Watch Series 3 or Apple Watch SE) • Altitude (Apple Watch SE and Apple Watch Series Only 6) • Favorite Contacts • Finding People • Heartbeat • Home • Email • Map • Message • Month • Music • News • Audio • Play Only • Phone • Podcast • Radio • Rain • Reminder • Remote Controller • Shortcut • Shortcut • Sleep • Stocks • Stocks • Stopwatch • Sunrise / Sunset • Time • UV Indicator • Voice Memo • Intercom (not available in all regions) • Weather • Weather • Wind • Exercise Avoca • Earth clock

X-Large

It should be when the largest mirror is needed. When you add problems, it fills the whole screen.

- Custom function: color
- Possible problems: events • alarms • air quality • audiobooks • batteries • blood oxygen (Apple Watch Series 6 only, not available in all regions) • breathing • counters • calendars • Camera remote controls • cell phones (models mobile-only) • Compass • Loop tracking • Date • ECG (not available in all regions or Apple Watch Series 3 or Apple Watch SE) • Altitude (Apple Watch SE and Apple Watch Series 6 only) • Favorite Contacts • Find People • Heart Rate • Family • Email • Map • Message • Month • Music • News • Audio • Phone • Podcast • Radio • Rain • Reminder • Remote control • Shortcut • Sleep • Stock • Stopwatch • Sunrise / Sunset • Time • UV indicator • Voice Memo • Intercom (not available in all regions) • Weather • Weather • Wind • Exercise • Earth Clock

Browse the gallery face on the Apple Watch

The face gallery in the Apple Watch app is an easy way to view all available clock faces. When you find an interesting emoji, you can customize it, choose a complex emoji, and add it to your collection - all from the gallery.

Open the face of the gallery

Open the Apple Watch app on your iPhone, and then tap Face Gallery.

Choose facial features

In "Face Gallery", tap the face, then tap the element, such as color or style.

If you use a variety of options, the divine appearance will change, so you can be sure that the make-up is right.

Add issues to "Face Gallery"

1. In "Face Gallery", tap the face, then tap a complex area, such as "top left", "top right", or "bottom".
2. Swipe to see local problems, then tap location.
3. If you decide you do not want problems in this area, scroll to the top of the list and click Close.

For a complete list of problems found on the face of each clock, check out the face of the Apple watch and its functions.

Add a face

1. After customizing the face in "Face Gallery", click "Apply".
2. To switch to a new face in Apple Watch, swipe left on the face of the clock until you see it.

Share the face of the Apple Watch

With watchOS 7, you can share the face of the clock with friends. Shared faces can include watchOS and problems created by third parties.

Note: The face clock receiver must also have an Apple Watch with watchOS 7.

Share the face of the clock

1. On the Apple Watch, show the face of the watch to be shared.
2. Touch and hold the display, then click the share button.
3. Click Add Contact to add recipients, then click Create Message to compose your message.
4. Tap the face of the clock face, then tap "Uninstall" to eliminate any issues you do not want to share.
5. Click Submit.

You can also open the Apple Watch app, tap the clock face from your favorites or Face Gallery, then tap the "Share" button, and select the sharing option.

Received a watch face

You can find the face of a shared watch sent to you by "message" or "post" or by clicking the online link.

1. Open the text, email, or link that contains the clock face shared.
2. Click the face of the shared clock, then click Insert.

If you find a watch with complex functions from a third-party app, please click the app price, or click download app in the App Store. You can also click "Continue without this program" to get a clock face without a third-party problem.

Custom the watch face

Customize your Apple Watch face to look the way you want it and provide the features you need. Choose a design, adjust colors and features, and add to your collection. Change faces at any time to see the right time tool — or move things.

The face gallery in the Apple Watch app is an easy way to view all existing clock faces, customize them and add them to your collection. However, if your iPhone is not easy to use, you can customize your face to the clock. For more details, see the face of the Apple Watch and its functions.

Choose a different clock face

- Swipe to the edge of the drive to view other locations in favorites.
- To view all available clock faces, touch and hold the clock face, swipe to the desired clock face, and then tap.

Increase dial difficulty

You can add special features (called problems) to some clock faces to quickly check items such as stock prices, weather reports, or information from other installed apps.

1. With the display face, touch and hold the display, then tap "Edit".
2. Swipe left to end.

If there are problems with the face, they will be displayed on the final screen.

3. Tap the problem to select it, then open "Digital Crown" to select a new task, such as "Activity" or "Heart Rate".
4. When you're done, press the digital crown to save your change, then tap the face to switch to that location.

Adding difficulty to other apps

In addition to the built-in problem displaying information such as weather, stocks, or news, you can add a problem to many of the problems you find in the App Store. To make these problems available when customizing faces, follow these steps:

1. Not built up the Apple Watch app on your iPhone.
2. Click on my watch, then click Problems.

Add a clock face to your collection

Create your custom face collection — even variations of the same design.

1. For the current clock face view, tap and hold the display.
2. Swipe left to the end then clicks the "New" (+) button.
3. Rotate the digital crown to browse the face of the clock, then click the face of the clock to be added.

After adding, you can customize the face of the clock.

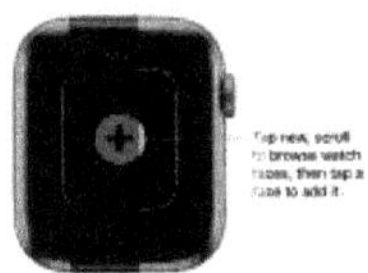

View your collection

You can see all the dials at a glance.

1. Not built up the Apple Watch app on your iPhone.
2. Tap "My View" and swipe your collection under "My Face."

To reset preferences, click "Reset" and drag the "Reset" icon next to the clock up or down.

Remove faces from your collection

1. For the current clock face view, tap and hold the display.
2. Swipe to the unwanted face, then swipe up and tap "Delete".

Or, on your iPhone, open the Apple Watch app, tap "My Watch", then tap "Edit" in the "My Face" area. Tap the "Delete" button next to the clock you want to remove, then tap "Delete."

You can add a clock face again at any time in the future.

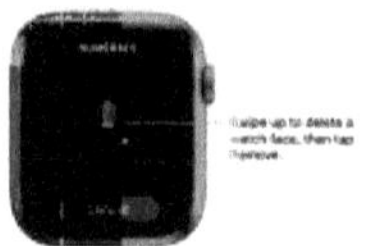

Put the clock in front

1. Not built up the "Settings" app on your Apple Watch.
2. Click on the clock.
3. Tap 0 minutes, then open the "digital crown" to upgrade the clock in 59 minutes.

This setting only modifies the time displayed on the clock - it will not affect the time on alarms, notices, or another time (such as a world clock).

Set up an Apple Watch for your family

Use the Apple Cash Family in the Apple Watch for a family member

If you are a family group organizer, you can set up Apple Cash for kids and teens in the family group so they can buy goods and send and earn money via Messages. You can also limit who your children can send money to, be alerted when they make a business deal, and lock their accounts.

For more information on system requirements and how to manage your Apple Cash account, please see the Apple Support article "Set up and use the Apple Cash series".

Note: Apple Cash is not available in all regions, and iPhone SE and iPhone 6 and above are also supported. For more information on using Apple Pay and Apple Cash, please refer to the iPhone User Guide

Setting up an Apple Cash family

To set up an Apple Cash Family, you must be a family planner.

1. On your iPhone, go to Settings> [your name]> Home Sharing.
2. Click "Apple Cash" and do one of the following:
    - If there are no children in your family group: Click "Create a children's account" and follow the instructions on the screen
    - If you have a child in your family group: Tap to set up Apple Cash, tap the child's name, and follow the instructions on the screen.

In the United States, your family can send and receive money in the messaging app and use Apple Pay to make purchases.

Manage Apple Cash in the Apple Watch for a family member

1. Open the e-wallet app on the iPhone used to manage the

clock.

2. Tap your Apple Cash card and then tap the "More" button.
3. Swipe up and tap the name under "Family."
4. Set the following options:
    - Choose who your family can send money to.
    - Select information when your family makes a transaction.
5. Tap [Remittance] to increase the balance of your family member.

To view family transactions, click on the action screen, or open the Wallet app on your iPhone, and then click your Apple Cash card. Your family activities will be displayed under "Recent Activity", and if you click "Activity" by [year].

Set reminders on your family's Apple Watch

Upgrade reminder

On an Apple Watch, you need to upgrade iCloud reminders to use other Siri connections, so you can create daily reminders (reminders are set for a specific day, not a specific time), and for others to add.

1. Open the "Settings" app on the managed Apple Watch.
2. Click the reminder, then click Upgrade.

Set notification time for all-day reminders

1. Open the "Settings" app on the managed Apple Watch.
2. Tap the reminder to turn on today's notification to show the time, then tap the time.
3. Enter the time you want the notification to appear, and then click "Set".

Choose a default list

On an Apple Watch managed, reminders made outside a specific list will be displayed in the default list.

1. Open the "Settings" app on the managed Apple Watch.
2. Click Reminder, and then click the current default list settings.
3. Click on the list you want to be the default list.

Observe the activities and health reports of family members

After setting the daily activity goal, you can see the level of daily activity for your family. With your family's permission, you can also view their health information.

Note: The objectives of children's work on the Apple Watch are different from the goals of adults. Exercise goals are based on minutes of exercise rather than calories. Exercise goals focus on minutes of fast-paced activities, such as running, jumping, and playing. If your child is under 13 years of age, outdoor running, cycling, and cycling exercises are designed for that age group.

View activity report

1. After setting your family activity goals, open the "Health" app on your iPhone.
2. Click Browse, and then click the name of your family member under Shared Health Data.
3. Click on an event.
4. Tap the timeline to see how much your family is doing at this time of day.

You can check event details for a day, week, month, or year.

View health information

If your family allows, you can view more information about

their activities and body measurements, health sensations, and heart rate details.

1. Open the "Health" app on your iPhone and click "Browse".
2. Under "Share health information," click the name of your family member.
3. Tap "Health Category" and then click a classification.

Enter medical information and medical ID

If you did not enter your family's health information during the setup process, please follow the steps below:

1. Open the Apple Watch app on the iPhone used to manage the clock.
2. Tap "All Views" and then tap the clock under "Family Views."
3. Click Finish, click Health, and perform any of the following actions.
   - Tap "Health Information" to enter or edit information, such as date of birth, length, and weight.
   - Tap on "Medical ID" to add emergency contacts, etc.

You can view health information and medical ID on the iPhone and the clock used to manage your Apple Watch.

- On your iPhone: Open the "Health" app, click "Browse", click the name of your family member, and click "Profile".
- In the Apple Watch managed: Open the Apple Watch app "Settings", then click "Health".

Set up an Apple Watch for family members

You can set up and manage the Apple Watch for people who do not have an iPhone (for example, your school children or parents). To do this, you must become a family planner or parent/guardian in the "Family Sharing" group.

The iPhone that was used to pair and set up the Apple Watch must be within the standard range of the Apple Watch Bluetooth (approximately 33 meters or 10 meters) to manage settings and software updates. Anyone who wants to set up an Apple Watch must be a member of the "Family Sharing" team and have an Apple Watch SE or Apple Watch Series 4 or higher that supports cell phones. (Your family member's watch does not require the use of a mobile phone manager with the iPhone that controls it.) For information on family sharing settings, please refer to the iPhone User Guide.

Using the Apple Watch app and "Screen Time" on your iPhone, you can manage the following:

- Communication restrictions
- Time on screen
- School-time-measuring performance of some Apple Watch activities during school hours
- Exposed content, purchases, and privacy restrictions

Additionally, you can also view the details of Apple Watch's "Activity", "Health" and "location" settings.

Note: The Apple Watch family member set is restricted from other communications with the iPhone used to set up family members. For example, you can't unlock a paired iPhone from an Apple Watch family member set, and you can't transfer tasks from an Apple Watch managed to an iPhone. If you uninstall an app from apps set by family members on your Apple Watch, the app will not be removed from the iPhone used to set up the app.

Set up an Apple Watch for your family

Setting up an Apple Watch for family members is the same as setting a watch. Before pairing and setting a family member's watch, wipe the clock to make sure it is empty.

1. Let your family wear the Apple Watch. Adjust the belt or choose the size of the belt so that the Apple Watch fits snugly but neatly on your wrist.

For details on changing the belt on the Apple Watch, see Delete, sunburn, and tighten the Apple Watch belt.

2. To open the Apple Watch, press and hold the sidebar until the Apple logo appears.
3. Place your iPhone next to the Apple Watch, wait for the Apple Watch pairing screen to appear on the iPhone, and then tap "Continue."

Or open the Apple Watch app on your iPhone, tap on "All Watches", then tap on "Pair New Watch".

4. Tap Set family members, then tap Continue on the next screen.
5. When prompted, place the iPhone so that the Apple Watch appears in the Apple Watch app's visual receiver. This will pair both devices.
6. Tap to set the Apple Watch. Please follow the instructions on the iPhone and Apple Watch to complete the setup.

For more information on setting up and pairing Apple Wa, see Setting and Pairing Apple Watch and iPhone.

Manage Apple Watch for family members

1. Open the Apple Watch app on the iPhone used to manage the clock.
2. Tap "All Views," then tap the clock under "Family Watches," and then tap "Done."

When you click "My View" to manage your watch, you will see a variety of settings, including the following:

Setting	Options
General	See updates, change language and

region and

reset Apple Watch.

Cell phone If not, please set a cell phone. See Install the

Apple Watch on your mobile app.

Accessibility Configure accessibility settings.

Emergencies Turn on or off the press and hold the button

on the side to call emergency personnel, as

well as add and change emergency contacts.

class time Set up a school plan. See Getting Started

During School Hours.

Time to find out Manage parental controls, learn about your

family screen time, and set limits.

Function Manage the feeling of suitability for new

users.

the app store Enable auto-download and update.

contact person Choose a trusted contact.

hand washing Manage limits and turn on or off the timer

for handwashing.

Health Enter or edit health information and

medical ID, view the

	health information of a person using Apple Watch managed (with appropriate permissions and settings), request to share health information, and opt-out of access to health data.
Heart	View the heart data of people using the Apple Watch managed (with appropriate permissions and settings), including heart rate, heart rate variation, heart rate rest, and average heart rate.
Message content	Select the call option and set a smart response.
Noise	Turn the volume up on or off and set the volume limit.
Picture	Select an album from the iPhone used to manage the watch, then select the number of photos that can be shown on the Apple Watch.
Wallet and Apple Pay	Set up Apple Cash.

Exercise Choose an exercise view.

Set screen time

Use "Screen Time" to configure the controls of family members' Apple Watch. With "Screen Time," you can set a time when you're not on the screen and restrict applications to contacts and your family members that they can use to communicate with your contacts. You can also limit iTunes Purchases and in-app purchases, explicit content and location information

To set screen time, follow these steps:

1. Open the Apple Watch app on the iPhone used to manage the clock.
2. Tap "All Views" and then tap the clock under "Family Views."
3. Tap Finish, tap Screen Time, tap Screen Time Settings and then tap Turn Screen Time.
4. Select the "Leisure Time", "Application Restrictions" and "Content and Privacy Restrictions" settings.

On this screen, you can also view the "Time Screen" activity report for your family clock.

Alternatively, you can open the "Settings" app on your iPhone, tap on "Screen Time", tap the name of a family member under the heading "Family", and select a setting.

Play music on a managed Apple Watch

If you are a member of a family sharing group with Apple Music family subscriptions, you can listen to Apple Music on your managed Apple Watch as long as you have Wi-Fi or mobile network connectivity.

1. Open the "Music" app on the managed Apple Watch and do any of the following.
    - Click on the library to browse music stored on Apple Watch.\
    - Click Listen Now to view your selected music based on your listening habits.
    - Tap Search then specifies or draw artists, albums, or playlists.

   Note: Graffiti is not available in all languages.
    - Tap the playlist created by Apple Music's editor for kids and teens.
    - Tap an album or playlist added to your Apple Watch.
2. Use the music controls in the "Music" app, the "Radio" and "Now Playing" apps to play and select music.

To learn how to add or remove music from Apple Watch, see Add Music to Apple Watch and Remove Music from Apple Watch.

Start using school time on the Apple Watch

School time reduces Apple Watch activities during school hours, allowing family members to focus.

Set school time

1. Open the Apple Watch app on the iPhone used to manage the clock.
2. Tap "All Views" and then tap the clock under "Family Views."
3. Click "Finish", then click on "School Time".

4. Open school time and click to schedule time.
5. Select the date and time you want to enable "School Time" on your watch.
6. If you want to set multiple schedules in one day (8:00 am to noon, then 1:00 pm), click Add time. For example, until 3:00 PM.

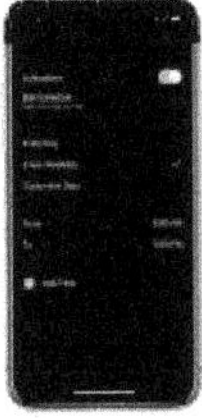

To change the next-class class schedule, open the Apple Watch app on your iPhone, click the "Info" button next to the control clock, click "Class hours", and then click "Set Schedule"

Time to drop out of school

Your family members may temporarily withdraw from "school time", for example watching the work ring.

Tap the display, open the "Digital Crown", and then tap "Exit".

If you leave during school time on time, dialing school time will return when you place your wrist. During casual hours, school time remains inactive until the next arranged time, or until you click the school time button in the Control Center.

Find out when you will open school time

When your family leaves school, you will receive a report telling them when and when they leave school. To view the report, please follow these steps:

1. Open the Apple Watch app on the iPhone used to manage the clock.
2. Tap "All Views" and then tap the clock under "Family Views."
3. Click "Finish", then click on "School Time".
4. Swipe up to view the report on the day, time, and dur-

ation of the school.

The report also appeared on Apple Watch. To view it, open the "Settings" app on your Apple Watch and tap School Time.

When the monitor goes to bed, school time will open again.

Tip: If school hours are not working, your family can open it, for example, if you join an after-school study group that is not on time and does not want to be interrupted. Just touch and hold down the screen, swipe up, and then tap the school button in the control center. To withdraw from school hours, please open the number crown. After opening school hours at the scheduled time or the Control Center, school time will be reopened.

Apple Fitness+

Download Apple Fitness + training on iPhone or iPad

You can download exercise content to your iPhone or iPad so you can exercise even offline.

1. Open the firmware application. After that, if you are using an iPhone, press Fitness +.
2. Do any of the following:
   - Download Exercise to Device: select Exercise, click the "Add Exercise" button to add the "My Exercises", then click the "Download" button.
   - View all downloaded exercises: Scroll down to the Fitness + tab and click on the downloaded exercises.

   To start downloading exercises, tap the desired exercise, then tap the button to start the exercise.

   - Remove downloaded tests from your device: Tap the "More" button, then tap "Uninstall download."

Note: The Heat Bar cannot be used during downloaded exercises.

About Apple Fitness +

After signing up for Apple Fitness +, you can access a fitness catalog, including cycling, strength, treadmill (running and walking), yoga, etc. When you exercise, your metrics (such as heart rate and calories burned) will be shared from Apple Watch to iPhone, iPad, or Apple TV, and will be synced with your daily activity details after completing the exercise.

Apple Fitness + requires Apple Watch Series 3 or higher with watchOS 7.2 or higher with one of the following Apple devices:

iPhone 6s or higher with iOS 14.3 or higher, and iPadOS 14.3 or higher iPad or Apple TV 4K with tvOS 14.3 or Apple TV HD or higher.

Note: Apple Fitness + is not available in all countries or regions.

Choose to exercise

When you need exercise, you have many options. To help you choose, you can view detailed information about each exercise, such as playlists and genre, whether the exercise is a closed caption or anything you need (such as dumbbells or mats). You can also check the activity before starting.

Find a coach

Each Apple Fitness + trainer brings his personality, musical taste, and fitness style. You can read the progress of each trainer and look at each trainer's exercise list in the "strength" app.

View your stats

During exercise, track the progress, heart rate, and calories used by each ring directly on your iPhone, iPad, or Apple TV.

Bicycle, HIIT, rowing, and treadmill exercises will also feature a "bar", which shows how your guide compares to other people who have exercised before. When you burn more calories, increase your calories in the "burner stick". Your position in the burning bar is maintained in the exercise summary and other indicators.

Pause and restart Apple Fitness +

You can pause the exercise from an exercise device or Apple Watch.

- On the Apple Watch, do any of the following:
  - Pause to exercise: Press the side button and Digital Crown simultaneously. You can also swipe to the right and tap "Pause."
  - Restart Exercise: Press the button next to "Digital Crown" simultaneously, or swipe right and click "Continue".
- For an iPhone or iPad, do any of the following:
  - Pause to exercise: Tap on the screen, then tap the pause button.
  - Resume: Click the "Play" button.
- On Apple TV:
  - Pause or resume exercise: In Siri Remote, press the touch area or press the "Play / Pause" button.

Sign up for Apple Fitness +

Apple Fitness + requires Apple Watch Series 3 or higher with watchOS 7.2 or higher with one of the following Apple devices: iPhone 6s or higher with iOS 14.3 or higher, and iPadOS 14.3 or higher iPad or Apple TV 4K with tvOS 14.3 or Apple TV HD or higher.

You can choose to integrate Apple Fitness + subscriptions with other Apple services by subscribing to Apple One Premier. See Apple support article Integrating Apple subscriptions with Apple One.

Note: Apple Fitness + and Apple One Premier are not available in all countries or regions.

Get the strength app

To use Apple Fitness +, you need the Fitness app on your iPhone, iPad, or Apple TV. If you do not have a fitness app on your device, you can download it from the App Store.

Sign up for Apple Fitness +

1. Open the solidarity app on your iPhone, iPad, or Apple TV. After that, if you are using an iPhone, press Fitness +.
2. Select the free trial button and follow the instructions on the screen to log in with your Apple ID and confirm your registration.

Cancel your Apple Fitness + subscription

1. Do any of the following:
   - On iPhone or iPad: Open the "Fitness" app, and, if you're using an iPhone, tap "Fitness +". Click the account button, click [account name], and then click Apple Fitness +.
   - On Apple TV: Open the "Settings" app, go to "Users and Accounts"> "[Account Name]"> "Subscriptions" and select "Apple Fitness +".
2. Follow the on-screen instructions to change or cancel your subscription.

If you are signing up for Apple Fitness + as part of an Apple One Premier subscription and want to cancel your subscription, please see the Apple support article on how to cancel a subscription from Apple.

Share your Apple Fitness + subscription with family sharing

When you sign up for Apple Fitness + or Apple One Premier, you can use "Family Sharing" to share your subscription with up to five other family members. Your family members don't have to do anything — as long as you have an Apple Watch Series 3 or higher, they can use Apple Fitness + for the first time when they open the Fitness app after you start registering. If family members have an Apple Watch but do not have an iPhone (because their Apple Watch is set by a family member), they can still use Apple Fitness + via Apple TV or iPad.

Note: To stop sharing your Apple Fitness + subscription with your family group, you can cancel your subscription, exit the family group, or (if you are a family group organizer) stop using family sharing.

Change the content on the screen during the Apple Fitness + workout

Change screen directions

During exercise, you can track the progress of each ring on the screen, as well as the heart rate and calories burned, all displayed on the device in real-time.

Some exercises also feature a "burn bar", which shows how your index compares to other indicators you've done before. When you burn more calories, increase your calories in the "burner stick". Your position in the burning bar is maintained in the exercise summary and other indicators.

You can change the screen directions from the Apple Watch you see on the screen during exercise. Reference settings will be synced between "firmware" applications on all devices signed in with your Apple ID.

1. During the exercise, click the "Indicators" button.
2. Do any of the following:
   - Close all indicators: Close "Display indicators".

Your metrics will still be collected, but will not be displayed on the screen.

- Change the time display method: select "turn off", "display the past tense" or "show the remaining time"

Closing "Time" will still show the time interval timer.

- Close the burning bar: close the burning bar.

If you turn off the "Burning Bar", your exercise will not help the Community Burn Bar, and you will not see where you are at the end of the exercise.

Open footnotes and footnotes

All Fitness + exercises support standard subtitles as well as audio and audio subtitles (SDH). After choosing a form of exercise, you can consider whether it includes closed captions and SDH under duration, type of music, and extra day.

- On iPhone or iPad: During exercise, tap the "Subtitles" button and select a language.
- On Apple TV: During the workout, swipe down the Siri Remote touch screen to display the "Information" window, then navigate to the "Subtitles" window and select a language.

Set up Apple Fitness + on Apple TV

Your Apple Watch can be synchronized with the Fitness app on Apple TV 4K or Apple TV HD for tvOS 14.3 or later, to use Apple Fitness + for exercise at the home, office, or on the go.

Connect your Apple Watch to Apple TV

To use Apple Fitness + and Apple TV, you need to connect an

Apple Watch.

1. Open the firmware app on Apple TV.
2. Choose your name, if you do not see your name, select Other.

If no one has signed in to your Apple TV, you may need to select "Login" in the "Fitness" app first.

3. On the Apple Watch, tap "Connect".

Note: You may need to open the "Workout" app on your Apple Watch in advance then tap "Connect".

4. When prompted, click "Continue" and enter the code from Apple TV to Apple Watch.

Note: To start exercising on Apple TV, your Apple Watch must be upgraded to watchOS 7.2 or higher, and Bluetooth must be turned on and off.

Choose who is exercising

If you use "Family Sharing", you can easily switch stuck between family members in the "Fitness" app on Apple TV. Friends or family members of Apple Fitness + subscribers outside the home-sharing group can use Apple TV to exercise.

1. Open the firmware app on Apple TV.
2. Choose your name, if you do not see your name, select Other.

If no one has signed in to your Apple TV, you may need to select "Login" in the "Fitness" app first.

3. To switch to a different family member or guest, select the account icon in the top left angle of the "Fitness" app, select "Sign Out", and then select another user.

Finish and watch the Apple Fitness + Workout

You can get rid of exercise from an exercise device or an Apple Watch.

After work is over, you can share exercise, cooling time, etc.

- On Apple Watch: Swipe right, then tap Finish.

  Show your exercise summary. Click Done to come back to the Workout app.

- On iPhone or iPad: Tap the "Finish" button, then tap "Finish exercising".

  Show your exercise summary. Click the Apply to Exercise button to add exercise to "My Workouts", click the share button to share the workout, click on "Cool Head" to select a workout, or click "Done" to return to Apple Fitness +.

- On Apple TV: Press the Menu button on Siri Remote, then select Finish Workout.

  Show your exercise summary. Select "Cool Head" to choose a cool workout, or select "Done" to return to Apple Fitness +.

You can watch a summary of the exercise again in the fitness app on your iPhone over time.

After taking the lesson, it will be displayed in the exercise list with the icon tagging icon.

Browse through Apple Fitness + Workout

Apple Fitness + can help you find the right form of exercise or exercise. You can browse for each exercise, start a multi-clip program, plan and refine certain types of exercises, or choose recommended exercises depending on your activities. The Mindful Cooldown workout starts in five minutes, all other forms of exercise start in ten minutes, and new exercises are added every week.

Browse the tests and get suggestions

Apple Fitness + recommends work-based exercise that often uses the "Workout" app on your Apple Watch and the apps you like to use with the "Health" app. Apple Fitness + will even recommend new trainers and exercises to help you improve your daily activities.

1. Open the solidarity app on your iPhone, iPad, or Apple TV. After that, if you are using an iPhone, press Fitness +.
2. Check out exercise and training:
   - Browse by type of exercise: Browse left or right to browse for a variety of exercises at the top of the screen.
   - Travel time (for iPhone only): Select the audio test you want to play on Apple Watch.

Click the "Add" button to add the "Walking Time" layout to Apple Watch. When you're ready to listen to the episode, open the "Workout" app on your Apple Watch and tap "Walk Time". Tap the "List" button, then open "Digital Crown" to scroll to other episodes on the Apple Watch.

- Browse the included tests: Navigate to categories such as "New This Week", "Beginner", "Popular" or "Easy and Quick".
- Browse to the trainer: Navigate down to the coach line, then scroll left or right and select the coach to view their performance, and then sort the performance by type, length, and type of music.

On an iPhone or iPad, click Show all to see a list of all the trainers.

- Many things to do: Browse your workouts with your regular trainers, as well as the types of exercises you do with the Apple Watch or other fitness apps that work with the Health app.
- Try something new: Check out exercises similar to the ones you've already done, but have different trainers

and recommended exercise types to balance your daily exercise routine.

- My Exercises (for iPhone and iPad only): Add exercises to "My Workout" from exercise details or exercise screenshots. My workouts can be used to keep a list of your favorite exercises, create exercise programs or keep playing exercises offline.
- Downloaded Exercises (for iPhone and iPad only): Exercises are downloaded to the device for playback offline.

Try more sets of eligibility programs

1. Open the solidarity app on your iPhone, iPad, or Apple TV. After that, if you are using an iPhone, press Fitness +.
2. Select an application.

Each program block shows the type of exercise and the number of episodes.

3. Do any of the following:
    - Preview Program: Select "Watch Movie" to watch a video about the program's objectives and types of exercise. You can also read details about the program to learn more.
    - Add episodes to "My Workout": select the "Apply" button next to the episode you want to add or select the "Apply All" button to add all episodes to "My Workout".
    - Start the layout from the system: select a layout from the list, then select a button to start the exercise.

To help you save your place after completing an episode, the next episode will automatically appear under "Next Workout", but you can select any episode at any time.

Filter and filter using

To get the exercise you want easily, you can filter and sort a specific type of exercise (such as rowing or dancing) by a trainer, length of exercise, type of music, etc.

1. Open the solidarity app on your iPhone, iPad, or Apple TV. After that, if you are using an iPhone, press Fitness +.
2. Choose a form of exercise, and do any of the following:
   - Sort tests: select "Filter" and then select an option, such as "Coach" or "Time".
   - Filter Exercise: Select "Filter" and select the filter you want to apply.

   If you can't select a filter, there are no tests for this filter.

When browsing, previous tests will display the "checkmark" icon in the icon.

Start Apple Fitness + training

start Apple Fitness + from your iPhone, iPad, or Apple TV. Apple Fitness + routine is open at all levels, so whether you're just starting or repeating your favorite exercises, you can still challenge yourself. For each of the exercises, some trainers will show exercise modifications to help you make exercise easier or more advanced. The trainer can also guide how to adjust the exercise, such as using weights instead of exercise blocks.

Start exercising on your iPhone or iPad

1. Open the firmware application. After that, if you are using an iPhone, press Fitness +.

If you do not have a fitness app on your device, you can download it from the App Store.

2. Select the type of exercise at the top of the screen, then select the exercise, or select an exercise from one of the categories (for example, "try new things").

To learn more about exercise programs, smart tips, etc. Check out the Apple Fitness + exercise.

3. Do any of the following:
    - Add My Exercise: Click the Add Workout button.
    - Preview Activity: Click Preview.

    You can also check out the playlist. When you sign up for Apple Music, click "Listen in Music" to open a playlist on Apple Music.

    - Start the exercise: Click the button to start the exercise, then click the "Play" button on your iPhone, iPad, or Apple Watch. If you want to start a printing press, select "run" or "walk" to get the most accurate reference.

    If you don't wear your Apple Watch, you can still start exercising, but your metrics (such as calories burned) will not be collected. Tap Exercise without looking to begin exercising.

    To stream exercise content to a compatible device with AirPlay 2.0 (such as a TV or HomePod), tap the screen during exercise, then tap the AirPlay button, and select your destination.

You can also start exercising on Apple TV. view the function below for more details.

Start working on Apple TV

1. Open the "Fitness" app and select an active person.

To learn more, see Setting up Apple Fitness + on Apple TV.

2. Choose a type of exercise, then choose an exercise, or choose an exercise in the category (for example, "try new things").

To learn more about exercise programs, smart tips, etc. Check out the Apple Fitness + exercise.

3. Do any of the following:
    - Preview function: select preview.
    - Start Exercise: If you have not registered, please select the free trial version button; if you are a subscriber, click the button to start exercising.

    If you want to start a printing press, select "run" or "walk" to get the most accurate reference.
    - Play selected songs from your "Music" workout: Navigate to the playlist and select a song to open the playlist in the "Music" app (Apple Music registration required).
    - Browse for related exercises: Scroll down to the "Related Exercise" line, then scroll left or right to browse for more exercises.

Basics

Set handwriting on Apple Watch

Apple Watch can detect when you start washing and encourage you to continue washing for 20 seconds, a time recommended by the Global Health Organization. If you do not wash your hands within minutes and return home, the Apple Watch will also let you know.

Turn on handwashing

1. Not built up the "Settings" app on your Apple Watch.
2. click Rinse Hands and open Hand Wash Timer.

When the Apple Watch finds out that you have started washing your hands, it will start the 20-second timer. If you stop washing clothes in less than 20 seconds, it is recommended that you complete the task.

Get hand-washing notifications

The Apple Watch may remind you to wash your hands shortly after returning home.

1. Not built up the Apple Watch app on your iPhone.
2. Tap on my watch, tap hands to wash and turn on hand-washing reminder.

Note: In the Apple Watch set for family members, you can also turn on hand-washing reminders. Open the ` ` Settings " app in the running Apple Watch, tap ` ` Hand Wash ", open ` ` Hand Wash Timer ", and open ` ` Hand Wash Reminder ".

For hand-washing reminders, you must set your home address

in "My Card" in the "Contacts" app on your iPhone.

To view the mid-time handwriting report, open the "Health" app on your iPhone, go to "Browse"> "Other Data", and then tap "Wash Hands".

Get more apps on Apple Watch

Your Apple Watch contains a variety of communication apps, health, fitness, and time. You can also choose to install third-party apps on your iPhone and find new apps in the App Store on your Apple Watch or iPhone. All your requests are on a single home screen.

Note: To automatically download the compatible iOS version of the app added to the Apple Watch, please go to "Settings" on iPhone, tap on "App Store", and enable "Automatic Download".

Find apps in the App Store on Apple Watch

1. Not built up the App Store app on Apple Watch.
2. Open the digital crown to browse the installed applications.

   Tap the category or tap "View All" at the bottom of the collection to see other apps.
3. To get the free app, click "Get". To purchase an app, click on the value.

   If you see the "Download" button instead of the price, it means you have already purchased the app and can download it again for free. Some apps require you to have some type of iOS app on your iPhone.

To find a specific application, tap the "Search" field at the top of the screen and use the call or enter the name of the application at will. You can also browse the app's custom sections by clicking on the section.

Note: If you are using an Apple Watch with a mobile phone, you may need to pay for mobile data. Graffiti is not available in all languages.

Install the apps you already have on your iPhone

By default, apps with watchOS apps available on the iPhone are automatically installed and displayed on the home screen. To choose to install a program instead, follow these steps:

1. Exposed the Apple Watch app on your iPhone.
2. Tap "My View", then tap "General", then turn off "Automatically install apps."
3. Tap my watch and scroll down to the available applications.
4. Click Install next to the program you want to install.

View and reply to notifications on Apple Watch

The app can send notices to keep you informed of meeting invitations, messages, audio notifications, and event reminders are just a few examples. The Apple Watch may display a notification when it arrives, but if you do not read that notice immediately, keep it for later review.

Warning: For important information about avoiding potential interference, see the Important Apple Watch Important Information.

Reply when a notification arrives

1. When you hear or hear a notification, raise your wrist to look at it.
2. Rotate the digital crown to scroll to the bottom of the notification, then click the button here.

You can also click the app icon in the notification to open

the consistent app.

3. To delete a notification, swipe down on it. Or scroll to the bottom of the notification and click Close.

View unanswered notifications

If you did not receive the notification, keep it in the notification center. A red dot above the clock face indicates that you have unread notifications. To view it, follow these steps:

1. Swipe down from the clock face to open the notification center. On some screens, touch and hold on to the top of the screen, then swipe down.

Note: When viewing the home screen on the Apple Watch, you cannot open the notification center. Instead, press Digital Crown to go to the clock face or open the app, and open the Notification Center.

2. Swipe up or down, or turn on Digital Crown to scroll through the notification list.
3. Tap notification to read or reply.

To clear an unread notification center, swipe left and tap X. To clear all notifications, scroll to the top of the screen and tap "Clear All."

When using group notifications, tap Group to unlock it, then tap the notification.

Tip: To avoid the red dot from appearing on the clock face, not built up the Settings app on the Apple Watch, tap Notifications, and turn off "Notice Identifier".

Choose how to send notifications

By default, app notification settings on the Apple Watch display settings on the iPhone. But you can customize the way other apps display notifications.

1. Exposed the Apple Watch app on your iPhone.
2. Tap My Clock, then tap Notification.
3. Click on an app (for example, Messages), click on Customize, and then select an option. Options may include:
    - Enable notifications: The app displays notifications in the notification center.
    - Send to notification center: The notification is sent directly to the notification center, and Apple Watch will not make a sound or display a notification.
    - Applications that support direct delivery to the notification center include "events", "breathing", "calendar", "email", "message", "podcast", "reminder", "intercom" and "wallet".
    - Notification off: The app is not sending any notifications.

You can also manage notification preferences directly on the Apple Watch by swiping left to notification and by tapping the

"More" button. Options may include:

- Silent delivery: notifications are sent directly to the notification center, and the Apple Watch will not hear or display notifications. To view and hear these alert notifications again, swipe to the left of the notification, tap the "More" button, then tap "Highlight."
- Turn off Apple Watch: The app does not send notifications.

Use notification collection

For each app on Apple Watch that supports notifications, you can choose how to collect notifications.

1. Exposed the Apple Watch app on your iPhone.
2. Tap My Clock, then tap Notification.
3. Click on the app, click on "Customize", then click on the "Notifications Group". Options include:
   - Closed: Notification collected.
   - Default: Apple Watch uses information in the app to create individual groups. For example, news alerts are organized by the channels you follow (CNN, Washington Post, and people).
   - By using: All app notifications have been collected.

Mute all notifications on Apple Watch

Touch and hold at the bottom of the screen, swipe up to open the control center, and then tap the silent mode button.

You will still feel tap when the notification arrives. To protect the sounds and taps, touch and hold down the screen, swipe over to open the control center, then tap the "Do Not Disturb" button.

Tip: When you receive a notification, you can quickly silence the Apple Watch by placing your hand on the viewing screen for at least three seconds. You will tap once to make sure the mute is turned on. Make sure Cover to Mute is on - Open the "Settings" app on your Apple Watch, then click on the "Sounds & Sounds" icons, then open Cover to Mute.

Turn off visually impaired notifications when the Apple Watch is locked

It doesn't matter if your Apple Watch is locked or unlocked, by default, Apple Watch will display a short notification - the name and icon of the notification app and the notification title on a single screen. You can choose to turn off small-eyed notifications when your Apple Watch is locked.

1. Not built up the "Settings" app on your Apple Watch.
2. Click "Notifications" and turn off "Always show a short look".

Keep notifications on Apple Watch private

When you lift your wrist to view a notification, you will see a quick snapshot and complete details in a few seconds. For example, when a message arrives, who will see you first, and then a message will appear. To stop displaying full notification without clicking on it, follow these steps:

1. Not built up the "Settings" app on your Apple Watch.
2. Click on notice, then open notification privacy.

Open the app on Apple Watch

The home screen lets you open any app on the Apple Watch. With Dock, you can quickly access frequently used apps. You can add up to Dock requests to save your favorites.

Show your app on a grid or list

The Home screen can display applications in grid or list view. To select one, follow these steps:

1. Not built up the "Settings" app on your Apple Watch.
2. click Application View, then Tap Grid View or Grade View.

You can also open the Apple Watch app on your iPhone, tap on "My Watch", tap on "App View", then tap on "Grid View" or "List View".

Open the app from the home screen

How you open the app depends on your viewing preferences.

- Grid view: Click the app icon. If you are already looking at the home screen, you can turn on Digital Crown to open the app in the center of the display.

- List view: Rotate Digital Crown, and then tap the app.

To return to the Home display from the app, press Digital Crown once, and then press again to switch to the clock face (or in the grid view, tap the view icon on the Home screen).

To quickly open the last application you used when viewing other apps or view faces, double-click the digital crown

Open the app from Dock

1. Press the sidebar, then open Digital Crown to scroll to apps in Dock.
2. Tap the app to open it.

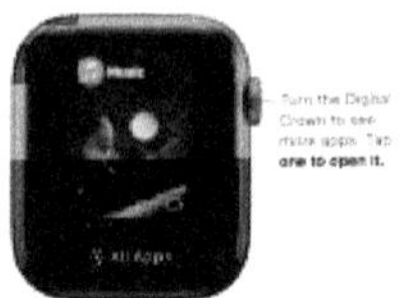

Choose which apps will appear in the dock

You can choose to show the most recently used apps in the Dock, or you can show up your favorite programs up to two.

- View recently used apps: Open the Apple Watch app on your iPhone, tap on "My Watch", tap on "Dock", then tap on "Recent". Recent applications are shown above the Door for the last time they opened, while other applications are shown below.
- Check your favorite apps: Open the Apple Watch app on your iPhone, tap "My Watch", and then tap "Dock". Select "Favorites", click "Edit", and then click the merge button next to the program you want to install. Drag the "Reset" icon to adjust its order.

If you select "Favorites", the recently used applications will be displayed on the top of the dock, allowing you to open them immediately. To add an app to Dock, click "Keep in Dock".

- To uninstall an application from Dock: Press the sidebar, then open Digital Crown in the program you want to uninstall. Swipe left in the app, then tap X.

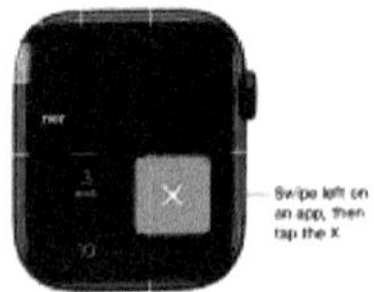

- Switch to the dock to the Home screen: Scroll to the

bottom of the dock and click on "All apps".

Tip: You can also add the most used applications to the face of the clock to increase its complexity. See the face of the custom clock.

Unlock Mac with Apple Watch

If you have macOS (mid-2013 or later) and macOS 10.13 or later, your Apple Watch can unlock your Mac as soon as it is asleep. You need to sign in to iCloud with the same Apple ID on your Mac and Apple Watch.

Tip: To find a model year for your Mac, click the Apple menu in the top left corner of the computer screen, and select About This Mac. The year of making the Mac is listed next to the model number, such as "MacBook Pro (15-inch, 2018)".

Turn on auto-opening

1. Make sure your device is set as follows:
    - Wi-Fi and Bluetooth are turned on on your Mac.
    - Your Mac and Apple Watch use the same Apple ID to access iCloud, and your Apple ID uses two-factor authentication.
    - Your Apple Watch uses a password.
2. On a Mac, select the menu "Apple"> "System Favorites."
3. Click Security & Privacy, and then tap General.
4. Select Use Apple Watch to unlock apps with Mac or Agree to Apple Watch to unlock Mac.

If you have multiple Apple watches, select the watch you want to use to open apps with the Mac.

If you did not agree to the two-factor verification in your Apple

ID, follow the instructions on the screen, then try checking the box again. Please see the Apple support article Two-factor authentication for Apple ID.

Unlock your Mac

When you enter your watch, you just need to wake up your Mac - no need to enter a password.

Tip: Make sure the Apple Watch is in your hand and unlocked, and that you are close to your Mac.

Use Siri on Apple Watch

Siri's helpful instructions

Siri can perform tasks and provide feedback directly on the Apple Watch. You can ask Siri to translate orally. Siri can see the songs and provide instant effects for Shazam. You can also ask Siri a common question, and the Apple Watch will show you the first search results and a brief quote on each page. Just click to open the page to view the page on the Apple Watch. Try asking Siri to do something that often requires you to complete a few steps.

Siri is not available in all districts and tongues. Please check the availability of the apple feature.

Ask Siri. Say this:

- "How do you say 'how are you?' In Chinese? "
- "Start running out of 30 minutes"
- "Tell Catherine I'm going to die"
- "Open sleep app"
- "What song is this?"
- "What causes a rainbow?"
- "What's my latest news?"
- "What can I ask you?"

Join Siri

To send a demand to Siri, do one of the following:

- Lift your wrist and talk on the Apple Watch.

To turn off the "Speak and Talk" feature, open the "Settings" app on your Apple Watch, tap Siri, and turn off "Talk and Talk".

- Say "Hello Siri" and state your request.

To turn off "Hey Siri", open the "Settings" app on your Apple Watch, tap Siri, and close to listen to "Hey Siri".

- Tap the Siri button on the face of the Siri clock.
- Press and hold the digital crown until you see the listening index, then speak your request.

To turn off the Press Digital Crown function, open the "Settings" app on your Apple Watch, tap Siri, and turn off Press Digital Crown.

Tip: After asking Siri a question, you can lower your wrist. When Siri answers, you'll feel a tap.

To answer Siri's questions or to continue the conversation, press and hold Digital Crown and speak.

Siri can answer you as it does on iOS, iPadOS, and macOS. You can also hear Siri through Bluetooth headsets or speakers connected to the Apple Watch.

Note: To use Siri, the Apple Watch must be connected to the Internet. Mobile charges may apply.

Change voice response settings

Siri could comment on the Apple Watch. Open the Settings app on your Apple Watch, tap Siri, and then select from the following options:

- Always available: Siri will respond even if your Apple Watch is in silent mode.
- Use silent mode to control: When the Apple Watch is set to silent mode, Siri will mute all voice responses.
- Headphones only: When the Apple Watch is connected to a Bluetooth headset, Siri will only speak the answer.

To modify the language and voice used by Siri, exposed the Settings app on your Apple Watch, tap Siri, and then tap Language or Siri Voice. When you tap Siri's voice, you can change the type and gender of the voice.

Delete Siri history

You can uninstall Siri integration and current calls that are compatible with Apple Watch from Apple servers.

1. Not built up the "Settings" app on your Apple Watch.
2. Tap Siri, tap Siri history, then tap Delete Siri history.

Unlock iPhone with Apple Watch

If you wear an Apple Watch (series 3 or higher), you can use it to cover your nose and mouth (iOS 14.5 or higher and watchOS 7.4 or higher) to securely unlock the iPhone model (with Face ID)).

To allow Apple Watch to unlock iPhone, do the following:

1. For iPhone, go to "Settings"> "Face ID and password".
2. Scroll down and open Apple Watch (under Apple Watch).

   If you have more than one clock, please open the settings for each clock.

3. To unlock the iPhone by closing your nose and mouth while wearing an Apple Watch, pick up the iPhone or tap its screen to wake it up, then look at the iPhone.

   Apple Watch is tapping your wrist to let you know that the iPhone is on.

Note: To unlock the iPhone, the Apple Watch must have a passcode, and it must be opened on the wrist and close to the iPhone.

Tell time on Apple Watch

There are several ways to tell you the time on the Apple Watch.

- Raise your wrist: Time comes from driving, clock in grid view, and the top right corner of most apps.
- Listening time: Open the "Settings" app on Apple Watch, tap "Clock", and open "Talk Time". Use two fingers to listen for driving time.

The Apple Watch can also play tones every hour. In the Apple Watch "Settings" app, tap "Clock" and open "Ringtones". Tap the sound to select "ringtone" or "bird sound".

- Feel Time: When Apple Watch is in silent mode, to feel the time spent on your wrist, open the "Settings" app on Apple Watch, click "Clock", "Taptic Time", "Taptic Time", and then select Options. See Use Taptic Time.

Note: If "Taptic Time" is disabled, Apple Watch may be set to talk time. To use "Taptic Time", first go to "Settings"> "Clock", then open "Silent Mode Control" under "Speak Time".

Ask Siri: Raise your wrist and say, "What time is it?

Link the Apple Watch to Bluetooth headphones or speakers

When the iPhone is not nearby, play audio from the Apple Watch on a Bluetooth headset or speaker.

Tip: If you have AirPods set for iPhone, you can use them with the Apple Watch — just press play.

Pair a Bluetooth headset or speaker

You need a Bluetooth headset or speaker to listen to great audio on Apple Watch (Siri, voice mail and voice memo played on Apple Watch). Follow the instructions that come with the headset or speakers to enter it in recovery mode. When the Bluetooth device is ready, follow the steps below:

1. Open the "Settings" app on your Apple Watch and tap "Bluetooth".
2. Tap the device when it appears.

You can also tap the "AirPlay" button on the "audiobook", "Music", "Now Playing", "Podcast" and "Radio" screen to turn on Bluetooth settings.

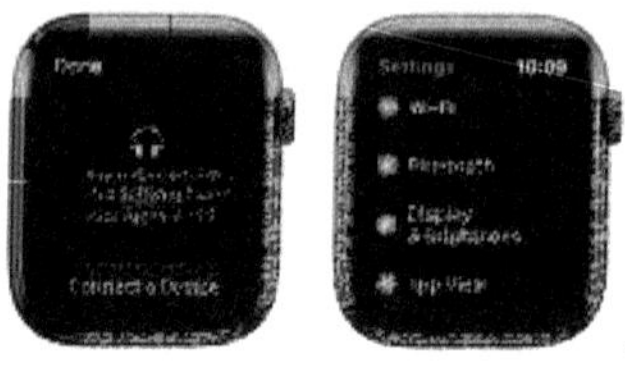

.

Select audio output

1. Touch and hold at the bottom of the screen, then swipe up to open the control center.
2. Tap the "Audio Output" icon and select the device you want to use.

For important details on avoiding ear loss, check out the Apple Watch safety key information.

Decrease loud noises

Apple Watch can limit earphone ringtones at set decibel levels.

1. Not built up the Settings app on your Apple Watch.
2. Go to Sound and Haptics, Headset Security, and click Moderate Sound.
3. Enable "Minimize noise" and set the level.

Get notifications about headphones

If you pay attention to loud noise over long headphones that can affect your hearing, Apple Watch (with watchOS 7.1 or later) can send you a notification and automatically lower the volume to the appropriate level to protect your hearing.

1. Open the "Settings" app on your iPhone.
2. Click "Sounds & Haptics", click on "Headset Security", and open "Headset Notifications".

Note: Depending on your country or region, "headphone notifications" may be turned on automatically. In some countries or regions, you may not be able to turn it off completely.

Shows the number of notifications you have received in the last six months.

3. To learn more about headset notifications, click 6 Months ago.

To view detailed information about earphone notifications on your iPhone, open the "Health" app and click "Browse", "Hearing", "Headphone Notifications" and "Notifications" too.

Use shortcuts in Apple Watch

The "Shortcut" app on Apple Watch lets you start tasks with just a tap. Using the shortcuts you created on your iPhone, you can quickly find your way home, create more than 25 playlists, and more. You can use shortcuts from the "Shortcuts" app, or you can add them to the clock face as complex tasks.

Note: Not all shortcuts on the iPhone are compatible with the Apple Watch.

Launch the shortcut

1. Open the shortcut app on the Apple Watch.
2. Click on the shortcut.

Enter a shortcut problem

1. Touch and hold more space, then click "Edit."
2. Swipe left on-screen"Problems" and then tap Problems.
3. Scroll to a shortcut, and select a shortcut.

Add some shortcuts to the Apple Watch

1. Open the "Shortcuts" program on your iPhone.
2. Tap the More button in the top right angle of the shortcut.
3. Tap the "More" button on the shortcut screen, then open the "Show on Apple Watch".

Use Apple Watch for mobile network

With the Apple Watch with a mobile phone and a mobile phone connection with the same network company as the iPhone, you can make calls, answer messages, use walkie-talkie, stream music and podcasts, receive notifications, and more, even if you don't have a phone. Your iPhone or Wi-Fi connection.

Note: Mobile service is not available for all regions or all operators.

Install the Apple Watch on your phone app

You can use the mobile service on Apple Watch by following the instructions on the initial setup. To activate the service over time, follow these steps:

1. Not built up the Apple Watch app on your iPhone.
2. Tap on my watch, then tap on the phone.

Follow the instructions to learn more about the network service plan and use your mobile phone to make your phone use your Apple Watch. See the Apple care article "Setting Mobile to Apple Watch".

Turn the phone on or off

The Apple Watch with mobile function uses the best network connection — when your iPhone is nearby, a Wi-Fi network or mobile connection you have previously connected to your iPhone. You can turn off the cell phone, for example, to save battery power. Just follow the steps below:

1. Touch and hold at the bottom of the screen, then swipe up to open the control center.
2. Click the "Honeycomb" button, then turn it off or on "Honeycomb".

When the Apple Watch has a mobile connection and the iPhone is not nearby, the mobile network button will turn green.

Note: Long-term use of the phone will consume a lot of battery power (for more details, see the Apple Watch General Battery Information website). In addition, some programs may not be updated without connecting to the iPhone.

Check the mobile signal strength

When connecting to a mobile network, try one of the following methods:

- Use Explorer dialing, which uses green dots to indicate mobile signal strength. Four points are good communication. One point is bad.
- Open a control center. The green dot on the top left shows the cellular connection status.
- Add bee problems to dialing.

Check mobile data usage

1. Not built up the Apple Watch app on your iPhone.
2. Tap on my watch, then tap on the phone.

Use AirPods on Apple Watch to listen to and respond to messages

Using "Announcement Messages", you can listen to messages via AirPods (AirPods Max, AirPods Pro, and AirPods 2n d generation; AirPods Max requires watchOS 7.3 or higher). If a message is received while the Apple Watch is locked with AirPod connected, a beep will ring and Siri will start reading this message.

Open the announcement message

1. Put AirPods in your ears (AirPods Pro and second-gen-

eration AirPods) or on your head (AirPods Max).
2. Pair with Apple Watch.
3. Open the "Settings" app on your Apple Watch, go to Siri> "Announce Messages", and enable "Announce Messages".

Temporarily close "Announcement News"

1. Touch and hold at the bottom of the screen, then swipe up to open the control center.
2. Click the "Announcement Message" button.

Tap the "Announce Message" key again to open it.

Note: If you delete AirPods, the "Announcement Message" button will be disabled.

Reply to voicemail

Say something like "Answer this good news."

Siri repeats what you said and asks for confirmation before sending a reply. (To send a reply without waiting for confirmation, open the "Settings" app on your Apple Watch, go to Siri> Announce Messages, and then open "Unverified Reply".)

Prevent Siri from reading messages

You can do any of the following:

- Say something like "stop" or "cancel".
- Press the digital crown (AirPods Max).

Note: When listening to a message, you can open the digital crown to change the volume.

- Press any power sensor (AirPods Pro).
- Double-click any of your AirPods (second generation).
- Remove one of your AirPods (generation of AirPods Pro and AirPods 2n d).

Use the Apple Watch without the iPhone paired

Use Apple Watch without iPhone

With Apple Watch having a mobile network function and an active network system, you can stay connected even if you are far away from your iPhone. On all other Apple Watch models, you can still perform certain tasks even if you leave your iPhone and are not connected to Wi-Fi.

- Listen to a melody on Apple Watch
- Pay attention to the podcasts on the Apple Watch
- Listen to audiobooks on Apple Watch
- Record and play vocal sound notes on Apple Watch
- Get on the bus and use your student ID
- Use clocks, world clocks, alarms, timers, and stop clocks
- Show photos in synced album
- Use Apple Pay to shop
- View existing calendar events on the Apple Watch
- Track your activity and exercise
- Check your heartbeat, adjust your sleep plan, measure oxygen levels in the blood, follow your reproductive cycle, relax and breathe
- Rate the noise level around you

Note: The Apple Watch has built-in GPS, you can get accurate distance information and speed information while exercising outside without a paired iPhone. The Apple 3 series, Apple Watch Series 4, and Apple Watch Series 5 also have a built-in barometric altimeter for more accurate/downward information. The always open alarm in the Apple Watch SE and Apple Watch Series 6 is more accurate and can show the length of your actual current time without delay.

When your Apple Watch is linked to Wi-Fi

Once your Apple Watch is connected to a Wi-Fi network, you can still perform the following tasks (even if your iPhone is turned off):

- Find apps in the App Store
- Send and receive messages via iMe sage
- Call on Apple Watch (if you have enabled Wi-Fi hotspots or want to make a FaceTime audio call and are in the Wi-Fi network range, you can call)
- Use a walkie talkie
- Transfer to music, podcasts, and audiobooks on Apple Watch
- Upload music to Apple Watch
- View current weather conditions
- Track your stock
- Use the Apple Watch to control your home
- Use third-party applications that support Wi-Fi connections

Your Apple Watch uses Bluetooth® wireless technology to connect to its paired iPhone and use the iPhone to perform many wireless functions. Your Apple Watch can set up its Wi-Fi network, or use a paired iPhone to connect to a Wi-Fi network that you have set up or connected to. For more info, view the Apple Support article "About Bluetooth, Wi-Fi, and Mobile Networks" on Apple Watch.

Create an emergency medical ID

Medical IDs provide personal information, which can be useful in emergencies, such as allergies and medical conditions. Your Apple Watch may display this information for use by your caregiver in an emergency.

Tip: For people 55 years and older, it is very important to have an emergency ID that includes your date of birth. The Apple Watch SE and Apple Watch Series 4 also later include fall detection, which automatically opens when you are over 55 years old (may also be open to users over the age of 18).

Set up your medical ID

1. Exposed the "Health" app on your iPhone.

2. Click on your profile picture in the top right corner, then click Medical ID.
3. Click "Get Started" and enter your details.

View your medical ID in the Apple Watch

1. In the Apple Watch, press and hold the sidebar until a slide appears.
2. Slog the "Medical ID" slider to the right.

If you can't view your Medical ID when you press and grip the side button on Apple Watch, please open the Apple Watch app on your iPhone and click "My Watch", "Health", "Medicine ID", " Edit ", then open" Display on Lock ". To hide your Medical ID when Apple Watch is locked, turn off "Show when Locked."

Tip: Add emergency contacts to your Medical ID. If Apple Watch makes an emergency SOS call to an emergency person, Apple Watch will notify you. See Make emergency calls on Apple Watch.

Manage fall detection on Apple Watch (Only Apple Watch SE and Apple Watch Series 4 and above)

Fall detection screen.

After enabling fall discovery, if Apple Watch SE or Apple Watch Series 4 or later experience a serious fall, it can help you link to emergency services and send messages to emergency contacts. If the Apple Watch finds a severe crash and you are silent for about a minute, it will automatically call emergency services.

If you enter your age when editing your Apple Watch or using the "Health" app, and you are over 55 years old, this feature is automatically enabled. However, anyone over the age of 18 can follow the steps below to unlock the fall in Apple Watch SE and Apple Watch Series 4 and later:

1. Not built up the "Settings" app on your Apple Watch.
2. Go to SOS> Fall Detection, and turn on Fall Detection.

Note: If you turn off the wrist detection function, even though the Apple Watch SE and Apple Watch Series 4 and later versions have had a strong impact and crash, they will not automatically make an emergency call.

You can also open the Apple Watch app on your iPhone, tap on "My Watch", tap on "Emergency SOS", and then open "Fall Detection".

Edit apps on Apple Watch

Reset your apps to grid view

1. On the Apple Watch, press Digital Crown to install the home screen.

   When the screen is in the list view, open the "Settings" app on your Apple Watch, tap "App View", and then tap "Grid View".

2. Press the digital crown, touch and hold the app until everyone is running, then drag it to a new location.

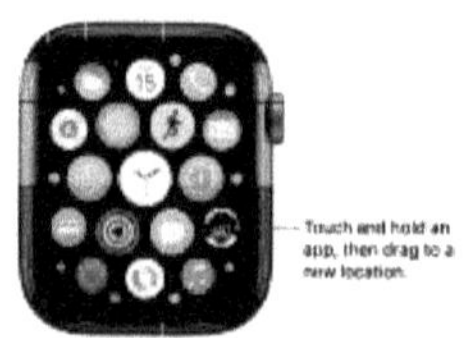

3. When you're done, click on Digital Crown.

   Or open the Apple Watch app on your iPhone, tap My View,

tap the app view, and then tap Edit. Touch and hold the app icon, then drag it to a new location.

Note: In the list view, applications are always arranged in alphabetical order.

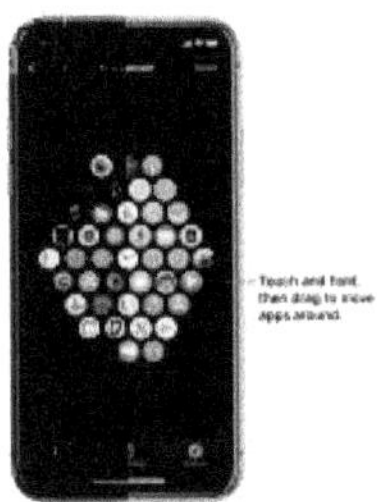

Remove apps from Apple Watch

- Grid view: On the Home screen, touch and hold the app icon until you see the X in the icon, then tap X to remove it from the Apple Watch. It will remain on the paired iPhone without even removing it.
- List view: Swipe the app to the left, then tap the "Trash Button" button to remove it from the Apple Watch. It will remain on the paired iPhone without even removing it.

Adjust app settings

1. Open the Apple Watch app on your iPhone.
2. Tap on my watch and scroll down to see the applications you have installed.
3. Tap the app to change its settings.

Some restrictions you have set on the iPhone "Settings"> "Screen Time"> "Content and Privacy Restrictions" will also affect Apple Watch. For example, if "Camera" is disabled on iPhone, the "Camera" icon will be removed from the Apple Watch home screen.

Check the last space used by the app

1. Not built up the "Settings" app on your Apple Watch.
2. Go to General> Usage.

Or open the Apple Watch app on your iPhone, tap My Watch, and go to General> Usage.

Connect the Apple Watch to a Wi-Fi network

By linking your Apple Watch to a Wi-Fi network, you can continue to use most of its purposes even if you don't have an iPhone.

Select Wi-Fi network

1. Not built up the "Settings" app on your Apple Watch.
2. Tap Wi-Fi, then tap the name of the available Wi-Fi network.

The Wi-Fi network compatible with Apple Watch is 802.11b / g / n 2.4GHz.

3. If the network requires a password, do one of the following:
   - Use your finger to type passwords on the screen. Use the digital crown to select uppercase or lowercase letters.
   - Tap the keyboard button and enter the password on another device.
   - Choose a password from the list.
4. Click to join.

Use a dedicated network address on Apple Watch

To help protect your privacy, Apple Watch uses a unique network address dedicated to each of the Wi-Fi networks you join, called Media Access Control Mode (MAC). If the network cannot use a secret address (for example, providing parental controls or marking your Apple Watch as authorized to join), you can stop using the network's private address.

1. Not built up the "Settings" app in AppleWatch your.
2. Click Wi-Fi, then click the name of the network you joined.
3. Close private addresses.

Important Note: For better privacy, please unlock "Private Address" in all networks that support private networks. Use a private address helps reduce Apple Watch tracking on different Wi-Fi networks.

Forget about network

1. Exposed the "Settings" app on your Apple Watch.
2. Click Wi-Fi, then click the name of the network you joined.
3. Click Forget this network.

If you join the network later, you must re-enter the network password.

Adjust brightness, text size, sound, and touch on Apple Watch

Adjust brightness and text on Apple Watch

Open the "Settings" app on the Apple Watch, then click "Show and light" to adjust the following:

- Brightness: Click the "Brightness" control to adjust, or click the slide, then open "Digital Crown".
- Text size: Tap the text size, then tap the letters or open the digital crown.
- Highlight: Open bold.

You can also make this adjustment on the iPhone. Open the Apple Watch app on your iPhone, tap My Watch, tap Display and Brightness, and adjust brightness and text.

Adjust the volume

1. Exposed the "Settings" app on your Apple Watch.
2. Click the sound and touch.
3. Click to control the volume under "Alarm Volume" or click the slide, then open "Digital Crown" to adjust.

Or, on the iPhone, open the Apple Watch app, tap "Sounds and Haptics," and drag the "Alarm Volume" slider.

You can also reduce the amount of noise from headphones connected to the Apple Watch. In Apple Watch's "Sound and Haptics" settings, click "Decrease Sound", then open "Decrease Sound".

Adjust the affected thickness

You can adjust the touch sensor or wrist tap power used by the Apple Watch to receive notifications and alarms.

1. Exposed the "Settings" app on your Apple Watch.
2. Click Sounds and Haptics, and not built up Haptic Warnings.
3. Choose default or highlight.

Or, on iPhone, open the Apple Watch app, tap "My Watch", tap "Sounds and Haptics," and select "Default" or "Highlight."

Turn on or off Digital Crown tactile function (for Apple Watch SE and Apple Watch Series 4 and above)

On the Apple Watch SE and the Apple Watch Series 4 and beyond, you will hear a click as you rotate the Drown Crown to scroll. To turn on or off this haptics, follow these steps:

1. Exposed the "Settings" app on your Apple Watch.
2. Tap "Sounds and Haptics," then open or close "Crown Haptics".

Or, on your iPhone, open the Apple Watch app, tap on "My Watch", tap on "Sounds and Haptics", and then turn on or off "Crown Haptics".

Use Taptic Time

When the Apple Watch is in silent mode, it can take time off the wrist with a series of different taps.

1. Not built up the "Settings" app on your Apple Watch.
2. Click "Clock", scroll up, and then click "Taptic Time".
3. Open "Taptic Time" and select the setting - "Number", "Short" or "Morse Code".

    - Numbers: The Apple Watch has a long press every 10 hours, followed by a short press per hour, a long press every 10 minutes, and then a short press every minute.
    - Concise: Apple Watch presses long once every five hours, press shortly once for the rest of the time, and then press long once every quarter.
    - Morse Code: The Apple Watch taps each digit of the time code into the Morse code.

You can also set Taptic Time on your iPhone. Open the Apple

Watch app on your iPhone, tap "My Watch", go to "Clock"> "Taptic Time", and then open it.

Note: If "Taptic Time" is disabled, Apple Watch may be set to talk time. To use "Taptic Time", first go to "Settings"> "Clock", then open "Silent Mode Control" under "Speak Time".

Provide functions from Apple Watch

The function of switching is to allow you to transfer from one object to another without focusing on what you are doing. For example, although you can reply to emails using the "Email" app on your Apple Watch, you may want to switch to your iPhone so you can use the on-screen keyboard to reply. The Apple Watch you have set can use Handoff, but the Apple Watch is set for family members not using it. Please follow the steps below to use "Handover".

1. Turn on your iPhone.
2. For an iPhone with Face ID, swipe up from the bottom edge and pause to show the App Switcher. (On iPhones with the "Home" button, double-click the "Home" button to display the app switch.)
3. Tap the button that appears at the bottom of the screen to open the same thing on the iPhone.

Tip: If you can't see the button in the App Switcher, please make sure "Handover" is turned on for your iPhone in "Settings"> "General"> "AirPlay and Handover".

By default, the switch is on. To disable it, open the Apple Watch app on your iPhone, tap on "My Watch", tap on "General", then turn off "Enable Toggle".

The switch function can be used in conjunction with events, alarms, calendars, family, email, maps, messages, music, news, calls, podcasts, reminders, settings, Siri, shares, stopwatches, timers, wallets, weather, and world watches. For Handoff to work properly, your Apple Watch must be connected to a paired iPhone.

If you have a Mac with OS X 10.10 or later, you can also switch from Apple Watch to Mac. For details on Mac-supported models, see Apple's support articles for Continuity on Mac, iPhone, iPad, iPod touch, and Apple Watch.

Apple Watch status icon

The status signs at the top of the screen give you information about the Apple Watch.

Status icon	What it means
	You have unread notifications. Swipe down on the face of the clock to read.
	Apple Watch is charging.
	Apple Watch battery low.
	Apple Watch is locked. Tap to enter the password and unlock.
	The water lock function is on, and the screen does not respond to the tap. Open the digital crown to unlock.

"Do not disturb" is turned on. Calls and alarms will not ring or light up the screen, but alarms are still active.

Flight mode is on. Wireless operation is off, but non-wireless functions are still available.

Theater mode is on. When you raise your wrist, the Apple Watch is muted and its display will not light up.

You exercise. To complete the exercise view Finish and watch the exercise on Apple Watch"

Apple Watch and mobile network lost connection to a mobile network. See Use Apple Watch for the mobile network.

Apple Watch has lost contact with its pair iPhone. This happens once the Apple Watch is not close to the iPhone, or when airplane mode is enabled on the iPhone. For more information, see the Apple support article If your Apple Watch is not connected or connected to the iPhone.

The Apple Watch is connected to its paired iPhone.

An app on Apple Watch uses location services.

The Apple Watch is connected to a well-known Wi-Fi network.

Wireless work or work process takes place.

The microphone is on.

The Apple Watch is connected to a mobile system. The number of points shows the strength of the signal.

Audio plays on Apple Watch. Click the icon to open "Now Playing".

The call continues. Tap the icon to open the "phone" app.

Sleep mode is on.

The map provides instructions. Tap the icon to open the "Maps" app.

You can now contact me via walkie-talkie. Tap the icon to not built up the "Intercom" program.

Use the Control Center on the Apple Watch

The control center gives you an easy way to check the battery, turn off the clock, turn on "Do not disturb", turn on the Apple Watch torch, put Apple Watch in airplane mode, turn on theater mode, and more unlock.

Open or close the control center

1. Open control center: Swipe up from driving. For some screens, touch and hold down the screen, then swipe up.

Note: You cannot open the control center on your Apple Watch home screen. Instead, press Digital Crown to go to the clock face or open the app, and open the Control Center.

2. Close by Control Center: Swipe down starting from the top of the display, or press Digital Crown.

Icon meaning

Turn on or off Apple Watch mobile models only on mobile phones.

Disconnect from Wi-Fi.

Unlock is only available for Apple Watch school models.

Put your iPhone on.

100% Check the battery charge percentage.

Mute Apple Watch.

Use a password to lock the clock.

Enable "Do Not Disturb".

Turn on sleep mode.

Let's use a walkie-talkie.

Open theater mode.

Turn on the water lock.

Turn on the flashlight.

Turn on airplane mode.

Select audio output.

Enable or disable "Announcement Messages".

Reset control center

You can rearrange the buttons in the Control Center by following the steps below:

1. Touch and hold at the end of the screen, then swipe up to open the control center.
2. Scroll to the ending of the Control Center and click "Edit".
3. Drag the button to a new location.
4. When you are done, click Finish.

Remove control center button

You can remove the "Control Center" button by following the

steps below:

1. Touch and hold at the end of the screen, then swipe up to open the control center.
2. Scroll to the ending of the Control Center and click "Edit".
3. Click the delete button in the corner of the button you want to delete.
4. When you are done, click Finish.

To restore a deleted button, open the control area, click "Edit", and then click the "Apply" button in the corner of the button you want to restore. When you are done, click Finish.

Turn on airplane mode

If you put the airline in airplane mode, other airlines will allow you to fly with your Apple Watch (and iPhone) unlocked. By default, airplane mode turns off Wi-Fi and mobile networks (for Apple Watch models with mobile networks) and keeps Bluetooth on. However, you can change the opening and closing settings when you switch flight mode.

- Turn on airplane mode in Apple Watch: touch and hold at the end of the screen, swipe up to open control center, and then tap the Flight mode button.

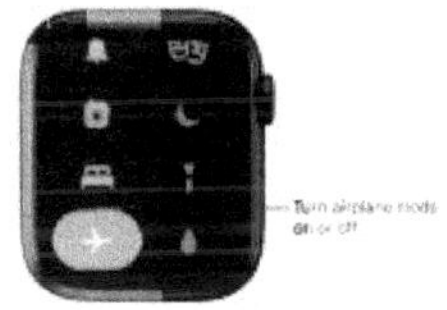

Ask Siri. Say something like: "Turn on plane mode."

- Install Apple Watch and iPhone in airplane mode in one step: Not built up the Apple Watch app on your iPhone, tap My Watch, go to General> Airplane Mode, and turn on Mirror iPhone. When your iPhone and Apple Watch are within standard Bluetooth range (approximately 33 meters or 10 meters) to each other, as long as you switch to airplane mode on one device, any other device will fit.

- Change the on or off airplane settings: In Apple Watch, open the "Settings" app, tap "Airplane Mode", and select to turn on or off Wi-Fi or Bluetooth automatically when you turn on airplane mode.

To turn on or off Wi-Fi or Bluetooth when Apple Watch is in airplane mode, open the Settings app and tap Wi-Fi or Bluetooth.

After enabling airplane mode, you will see an airplane mode icon at the top of the screen.

Note: Even if the Mirror iPhone is turned on, airplane mode must be turned off on iPhone and Apple Watch respectively.

Use the flashlight on the Apple Watch

Use a flashlight to illuminate the locks on dark doors, remind others when you are going out at night, or light up nearby objects while keeping a vision at night.

- Turn on the flashlight: Touch and hold the bottom of the screen, swipe up to open the "Control Center," and then tap the "Flashlight" button. Swipe left to select a mode-steady white light, bright white light, or a stable red light.
- Turn off the flashlight: Press the digital crown or side switch, or swipe down from the top of the dial.

Use theater mode in Apple Watch

Theater mode prevents you from opening the Apple Watch display when you lift your wrist, so it stays dark. It will also open the silent mode and make the "Intercom" status unavailable, but you will still receive relevant notifications.

Touch and hold at the bottom of the screen, swipe up to open control center, tap the theater mode button, and then tap theater mode.

After enabling theater mode, you will see a theatrical mode status icon at the top of the screen.

To activate the Apple Watch when the theater mode is on, tap the display, press the digital crown or side button, or open the digital crown.

Disconnect Wi-Fi

You can temporarily disconnect from the Wi-Fi network, and for Apple Watch models with mobile functionality, you can use the existing mobile connection directly from the Control Center.

Touch and hold the bottom of the screen, swipe up to open the "Control Center", and then tap the Wi-Fi button on the "Control Center".

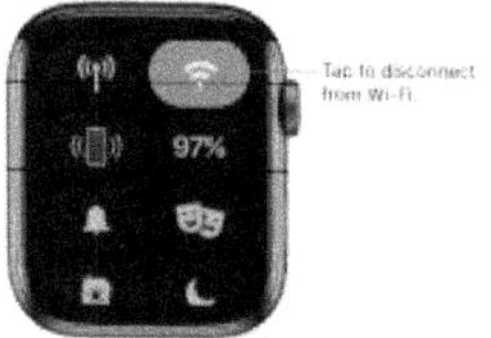

Your Apple Watch has been temporarily disconnected from the Wi-Fi network. If you have an Apple Watch with a mobile network, the mobile network connection will be activated when connected. When you leave and return to the location where you are connected to Wi-Fi, your Apple Watch will automatically join the network again without you forgetting it on your iPhone.

Turn on silent mode

Touch and hold at the bottom of the screen, swipe up to open the control center, and then tap the silent mode button.

Note: When your Apple Watch is charging, the alarm and timer will still sound or in silent mode.

You can also open the Apple Watch app on your iPhone, tap on "My Watch", tap on "Sounds and Haptics", and turn on silent mode.

Tip: When you receive a notification, you can quickly silence the Apple Watch by placing your hand on the viewing screen for at least three seconds. You will tap once to make sure the mute is turned on. Be sure to open the cover to mute the Apple Watch app on your iPhone, then tap "My View" and go to "Sounds and Haptics."

Open without interrupting

Use "Do Not Disturb" to prevent calls and alarms (other than alarms and heart notifications) from making sounds or lighting the screen.

You can turn on "Do Not Disturb" for a while until you leave your location or the calendar event ends. Just touch and hold the bottom of the screen, swipe up to open the control center, click the "Do Not Disturb" button, then select the options: Exposed, Open for 1 hour, Open until tonight, Open until I'm gone, And not built up till the end events.

You can also open the "Settings" app on your Apple Watch, click "Do Not Disturb", and then open "Do Not Disturb".

To automatically turn on "Do Not Disturb" when you start exercising, open the "Settings" app on your Apple Watch, tap "Do

Not Disturb", and enable "Do Not Disturb" You can also open the Apple Watch app on your iPhone, go to "General"> "Do Not Disturb", and enable "Do Not Disturb".

When Do Not Disturb is enabled, you will see a Do Not Disturb icon at the top of the screen.

Tip: To mute both Apple Watch and iPhone, open the Apple Watch app on your iPhone, tap My Watch, go to General> Do Not Disturb, and then open Mirror iPhone. After that, whenever you change "Do Not Disturb", other changes will fit.

Turn on or off sleep mode

Sleep mode features a simplified clock face and enables "Do not disturb". Normally sleep mode is turned off automatically depending on the sleep mode you created, but you can control it in the control center. Just touch and hold the bottom of the screen, swipe up to open the "Control Center", and then tap the "Sleep Mode" button. You can temporarily exit sleep mode by turning on Digital Crown to unlock. See Use the Apple Watch to track sleep for more information on sleep patterns.

Get your iPhone

Your Apple Watch can help you find nearby iPhones.

Touch and hold the bottom of the screen, swipe up to open the "Control Center," and tap the "Ping iPhone" button.

Your iPhone will make a sound so you can follow it.

Warning: in the dark? Touch and hold the Ping iPhone button, and the iPhone will light up. If your iPhone is not covered by the Apple Watch, please try "Find My Items" on iCloud.com.

In the control center, the Ping iPhone button is displayed in the middle left.

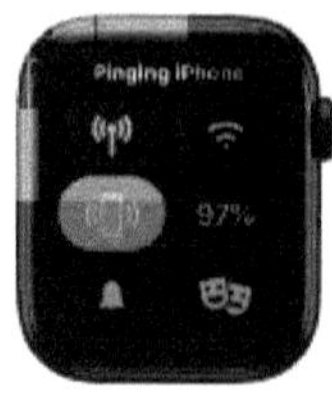

Get your Apple Watch

If you lose your watch, please use "Find My View" to recover it.

1. Open the "Find My" app on your iPhone.
2. Tap this device, then tap the clock from the list.

You can play a sound on your watch, tap on "Direction" to view its direction in "Map", and mark it as lost or deleted.

You can also use "Find Me" and "iCloud" to track Apple Watch. If your Apple Watch is lost or stolen, please refer to the "Find Apple Apple" and "Apple Support" articles.

Restart, reset, restore, and update

If you forgot your Apple Watch password

If your Apple Watch has been disabled because you forgot your password or entered too many incorrect passwords, you can use the Apple Watch app on your iPhone to reset your password. If you don't remember your password, you can reset your Apple Watch, reset your password, and restore your Apple Watch to backup. Restoring will delete content and settings from the Apple Watch, but will use a backup to enter your data and settings.

Important Note: Once the data is deleted, the data on Apple Watch will be erased after 10 failed password attempts.

Restart the Apple Watch

If it doesn't work, try restarting your Apple Watch and its paired iPhone.

Restart the Apple Watch

- Turn off Apple Watch: Press and hold the sidebar until the slide appears, then drag the "Power Off" slider to the right.
- Open Apple Watch: Press and hold the sidebar until the Apple logo appears.

Note: The Apple Watch cannot be restarted while charging.

Restart the paired iPhone

- Turn off iPhone: For models with Face ID, press and hold the sidebar and volume button, then drag the slider to the right. For models without Face ID, press and hold the side or up button until a slide appears, then drag the slide to the right. In any model, you can also go to "Settings"> "General"> "Off".
- Unlock iPhone: Press and hold the side or up button

until the Apple logo appears.

Force the Apple Watch to restart

If you are unable to turn off your Apple Watch or the problem persists, you may need to force restart your Apple Watch. Do this only if you can restart your Apple Watch.

To force a restart, press and grip the sidebar with Digital Crown at an equal time for at least ten seconds until the Apple logo appears.

Restore the Apple Watch from backup

Your Apple Watch will be automatically backed up to a paired iPhone, and you can restore it from a backup. If you back up your iPhone to iCloud or Mac or PC, install the Apple Watch backup. If your backup is stored in iCloud, you will not be able to view the information in it.

Back up and restore the Apple Watch

- Apple Watch Backup: After pairing with an iPhone, Apple Watch content will be backed up continuously on the iPhone. If the device is not paired, a backup will be done first.

For more info, view the Apple support article "Backing Up Apple Watch".

- Restore Apple Watch from backup: If you pair your Apple Watch with the same iPhone and, or get a new Apple Watch, you can select "Restore from Backup" and select the backup stored on your iPhone.

Once the clock is connected to a power source and Wi-Fi network, the Apple Watch owned by a family member will be backed up directly to the family member's iCloud account. To disable the iCloud backup of this watch, open the "Settings" app on the running Apple Watch, go to [account name]> "iCloud"> "Cloud Backup", and turn off "iCloud Backup".

Update Apple Watch software

You can update Apple Watch software by checking for updates to the Apple Watch app on your iPhone.

Check and install software updates

1. Exposed the Apple Watch app on your iPhone.
2. Click "My Watch", go to "General"> "Software Update", and, if any update is available, click "Download and Install."

Wipe the Apple Watch

In some cases, for example, if you forget your password, you may need to delete your Apple Watch.

Remove Apple Watch and Settings

1. Not built up the "Settings" app on your Apple Watch.
2. Go to General> Reset, click Clear all content and settings, and enter a password.

If your Apple Watch has a mobile network application, you can choose between two options: Erase everything and clear everything and save the app. To completely erase the Apple Watch, select Delete All. If you want to delete and restore it to the correct mobile network settings, select "Erase everything and save the application."

You can also open the Apple Watch app on your iPhone, tap on "My Watch", go to "General"> "Reset", then tap on "Clear Apple Watch content and settings".

If you can't access the "Settings" app on your Apple Watch because you forgot your password, place your Apple Watch on the charger and press and hold the sidebar until you see "Power Off". Press and hold Digital Crown, then tap "Reset".

After the reset is complete and Apple Watch restarts, you need to pair the Apple Watch with the iPhone and open the Apple app watch on iPhone and follow the instructions shown on the iPhone and Apple Watch.

Delete your mobile app

If you have an Apple Watch with a mobile network, you can delete the mobile network application at any time.

1. Exposed the Apple Watch app on your iPhone.
2. Click on my watch, click on the phone, and click the info button next to the phone app.
3. Click on the program removal [driver name], and confirm your choice.

You may need to contact your carrier to remove it from your phone.

Accessibility and related settings

Apple Watch access shortcuts

You can set Digital Crown to turn on or off VoiceOver with a third click, zoom in or touch the "fit" function.

Set access shortcuts

1. Not built up the "Settings" app on your Apple Watch.
2. Go to "Accessibility"> "Accessibility shortcuts" and select "VoiceOver", "Zoom" or "Touch Location".

You can also open the Apple Watch app on your iPhone, tap My Views, go to Accessibility> Access Shortcuts, and select an option.

Use shortcuts

Press the digital crown three times quickly. Double-click Digital Crown and turn off the accessibility function.

Set and use RTT on Apple Watch (only for mobile models)

Real-time text (RTT) is a protocol that transmits sound as you type text. If you have hearing or speech problems, the Apple Watch with a mobile phone can communicate using RTT when you are away from your iPhone. Apple Watch uses the built-in RTT software that you configure for the Apple Watch app and does not require any additional equipment.

Important note: Not all operators or all regions support RTT. When making an emergency call in the United States, the Apple Watch will send special letters or sounds to remind operators. The operator's ability to receive or respond to these tones may vary according to location. Apple does not guarantee that subscribers can answer or respond to RTT calls.

Turn on RTT

1. Exposed the Apple Watch app on your iPhone.

2. Tap My Clock, go to Access> RTT, and turn on RTT.
3. Click on the trunk number, then enter the phone number used to make the trunk call using RTT.
4. Enable Quick Send to send all characters as you type. Before sending, please close to complete the message.

Launch RTT call

1. Not built up the "phone" app on your Apple Watch.
2. Tap Contacts, then open the digital crown to scroll.
3. Click the contact you need to call, scroll up, and then tap the RTT button.
4. Doodle message, tap feedback from the list or send emoji.

Note: Graffiti is not available in all languages.

Text is displayed on the Apple Watch, similar to a "message" chat.

Note: If the other person on the phone does not have RTT, they will be notified.

Answer RTT calls

1. When you hear or hear a call notification, lift your wrist to see who is in the call.
2. Click the "Reply" button, scroll up, and then click the "RTT" button.
3. Doodle message, tap feedback from the list or send emoji.

Note: Graffiti is not available in all languages.

Set the default answer

If you are making or receiving an RTT call on an Apple Watch, just tap to send a response. To create more responses, follow these steps:

1. Exposed the Apple Watch app on your iPhone.
2. Tap "My View", go to "Accessibility"> "RTT", then tap on

"Automatic Reply."

3. Click "Enter Response", enter your response, and then click "Finish".

Tip: Usually the answer ends with "GA" and you can continue. It tells others that you are ready to accept their response.

To edit or delete existing responses or change the order of answers, click Edit on the default answers screen.

Adjust text size and other visual settings in the Apple Watch

You can correct the text size and other settings to simply interact with the features on the screen.

Adjust text size

You can change the text size displayed in any location that supports "Dynamic Type" (such as the "Settings" program).

1. Not built up the "Settings" app on your Apple Watch.
2. Go to Display and light, Text size then opens Crown Digital to adjust.

Choose how the text and other items are displayed

You can set text to be bold, use grayscale, and you can set other choices to change the look of an object on the screen. Open the ` ` Settings' app in your Apple Watch, tap ` ` Accessibility ", and then open or close the following options:

- Outstanding
- Label

Open the button label to see more position indicators. After enabling the label, you will see one (1) in the open option and zero (0) in the closed option.

- Gray
- Reduce visibility

Openness will increase readability in certain situations.

You can also open the Apple Watch app on your iPhone, tap on "My View", tap "Accessibility", and change the options.

Note: Restart the Apple Watch for bright and gray text changes.

Restrict animation

You can limit the actions you see on the home screen when you open and close apps.

1. Exposed the "Settings" app in Apple Watch your.
2. Go to "Accessibility"> "Decrease Action" and enable "Decrease Action".

You can also open the Apple Watch app on your iPhone, tap My Watch, go to Accessibility> Reduce Exercise, and open Reduce Exercise.

Tip: When "Reduce Movement" is enabled and the grid view is selected for the home screen, all app icons are equal.

The basics of Apple Watch with VoiceOver

With VoiceOver on Apple Watch, you can carry out many tasks by pressing, swiping, or turning on Digital Crown. Try the following when looking at the face of the current clock.

- Change the face of the clock: Press firmly on the display, then swipe left or right with two fingers to browse the available clock face. When you find someone you like, double-tap to select him.
- Custom face clock: Press the indicator firmly, swipe down to select "Custom", and double-tap. Swipe left or right to browse for custom functions. Rotate the digital crown to customize the selected function. When you're done, click on Digital Crown and double-click to save your changes.
- View notifications on the clock face: Swipe down with two fingers.

To view notifications from many other screens, tap the

time in the top right corner of the screen, then swipe down with two fingers.

- Open the "Control Center" on the face of the clock: Swipe up with two fingers.
- To open Control Center from many other screens, tap the time in the top right corner of the screen, then swipe up with two fingers.

Open Dock: Press the sidebar, then open Digital Crown to browse your favorite apps. Double-click the app to open it.

- Open any app: Press the digital crown and install the home screen. Swipe left or right, tap or drag your finger to highlight an app, then double-tap to open it. Or let Siri open it for you: press and hold Digital Crown until you double-click, then say "Get Started" and then the application name (for example, "Start Email").
- Read emails: Press the digital crown and insert the home screen. Swipe to highlight the "Mail" program, then double-tap (or press and hold Digital Crown and let Siri "start email"). After the mail application is open, swipe left or right to read the post.
- Use "digital crown" to navigate: tap three times with two fingers, then open the "digital crown" to select an item. Use two fingers to press three times to close the digital crown navigation.

Use VoiceOver to set up an Apple Watch

VoiceOver can help you set up your Apple Watch and connect it to your iPhone. To make VoiceOver speak, touch and hold the display, then move your finger back and forth to swipe left or right. Double-click to activate highlighted object. For details on using VoiceOver on Apple Watch, see using VoiceOver on Apple Watch.

Use VoiceOver to set up an Apple Watch

1. If your Apple Watch is not unlocked, press and hold the

sidebar (available under Digital Crown) to unlock it.
2. On Apple Watch, open VoiceOver by double-clicking on Digital Crown.
3. Move the iPhone next to the Apple Watch.
4. On your iPhone, select "Continue" and double-tap.
5. On your iPhone, tap "Set Apple Watch" and double-tap.
6. To try automatic pairing, point the iPhone camera at least 6 inches from the clock.

When you hear a pairing confirmation message, follow the voice instructions. If you have a problem, you can try pairing by hand; please follow steps 7 to 13.

7. On your iPhone, select "Pair Apple Watch Manually" and double-tap.
8. In the Apple Watch, select the "Information" button in the lower-right corner, then double-tap.
9. On your Apple Watch, select the Apple Watch ID near the top of the screen. You will hear a unique Apple Watch identifier, such as the "Apple Watch 52345".
10. On your iPhone, select the same identifier and double-tap.
11. Choose a six-digit pairing code on the Apple Watch to hear it.
12. Use the keyboard to enter the pairing code from Apple Watch to iPhone.

After the pairing is successful, you will feel a tap from Apple Watch and hear "Your Apple Watch is paired." If the match fails, click to reply to the alert. The Apple Watch and Apple Watch apps on your iPhone will be reset, so try again.

13. On your iPhone, select "Restore from backup" or "Set as new Apple Watch" and double-tap.
14. Follow the voice instructions to proceed with setting up the Apple Watch.

After completing the settings, the Apple Watch will be synchronized with the iPhone. This will take some time, please tap "Sync Progress" on your iPhone to see the progress. When you hear "Full Sync", your Apple Watch is ready to display the face of the clock. Swipe left or right to browse view face features.

Apps

Measure blood oxygen level in Apple Watch (applies to Apple Watch Series 6 only)

Use the Blood Oxygen app in the Apple Watch Series 6 to measure the percentage of oxygen carried by red blood cells from the lungs to other parts of the body. Knowing the level of oxidation in the blood can help you understand for the rest of your life.

Note: The blood oxygen application is not available in all regions. The dose of oxygen application is not suitable for medical use.

Set blood oxygen

1. Open the Apple Watch app on your iPhone (iPhone 6s or the latest iOS 14).
2. Tap my watch, tap blood oxygen, and turn on the blood oxygen level.

Turn off the background measurement in sleep mode and theater mode

The blood oxygen level uses a bright red light that shines on your wrist, which can be most noticeable in dark areas. If you experience light disturbance, you can close the scale.

1. Exposed the "Settings" app on your Apple Watch.
2. Tap the blood for oxygen, and turn it off in "Sleep Mode" and "Theater Mode".

Measure your blood oxygen level

When the back measurement function is turned on, the blood oxygen app will always measure your blood oxygen level throughout the day, but you can also take the required doses at any time.

1. Not built up the Blood Oxygen app on the Apple Watch.
2. Place your arms on a table or knee and make sure your wrists are flat and the Apple Watch display is facing upwards.
3. Tap Start, then hold your arm smoothly during the 15-second countdown.
4. At the end of the scale, you will get the result. Click Finish.

Note: For best results, the back of the Apple Watch requires a skin connection. Do not wear the Apple Watch firmly or freely, so that the skin has a place to breathe, which helps ensure an effective measure of oxygenated blood. For more details, check out the Apple Support Oxygen App article in the Apple Watch Series 6 that measures your blood oxygen level.

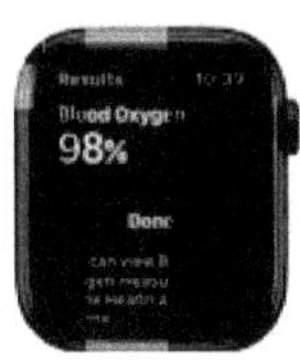

View your blood oxygen balance records

1. Open the "Health" app on your iPhone.
2. Click Browse, click Breath, and then click Blood Oxygen.

Use the ECG app to record ECG on Apple Watch

The Apple Watch Series 4 also later has an electronic heartbeat sensor, as well as an ECG app, which allows you to record an electrocardiogram (or ECG). To use the ECG app, please keep informed your iPhone 6s or later to the latest iOS version, and update your Apple Watch to the latest version of watchOS. ECG applications are not available in all regions.

1. Open the "Health" app on your iPhone and follow the steps on the screen to set the ECG.

   If you are not told to set a reminder, please click "Browse" in the lower right corner, click "Heart", then click on "Electrocardiogram (ECG)".
2. Open the ECG program on the Apple Watch.
3. Place your arms on a table or knee.
4. Put your hand on the other side of the clock, place your finger on the Digital Crown, and wait while the Apple Watch records the ECG.

You do not need to press Digital Crown during the meeting.

At the end of the recording, you will receive a split. After that, you can click on "Apply" and select your brand. Click "Save" to record any symbols, then click "Finish". To view results on your iPhone, open the "Health" app on your iPhone, click "Browse" in the lower right corner, and click "Heart"> "Electrocardiogram (ECG)".

Check your heartbeat on the Apple Watch

A heartbeat is an important means of monitoring body condition. You can check your heartbeat during exercise; check rest, walking, breathing, exercise, and recovery rate throughout the day; or re-read at any time.

Examine your heart rate

Open the "Heart Rate" app on the Apple Watch to view current heart rate, rest rate, and normal walking rate.

As long as you wear an Apple Watch, the Apple Watch will continue to measure your heart rate.

Check your heart rate during exercise

By default, your current heart rate is displayed in the “multi-indicator” exercise view. To customize the indicators from the exercise session, follow these steps:

1. Exposed the Apple Watch app on your iPhone.
2. Tap "My View", go to "Workout"> "Workout View", then tap Exercise.

For more information, see Start Exercising on the Apple Watch.

View your heart rate data graph

1. Not built up the "Health" app on your iPhone.
2. Click "Browse" at the bottom right, click "Heart Rate", and then click "Heart Rate".
3. To add "Heart Rate" to "Summary", swipe up and click "Add to Favorites."

You can view heart rate for hour, day, week, month, or a year ago. Click to show more heart rate data, and you can view your heart rate range at a selected time; your rest, moderate walking, exercise, and breathing rate; and any high or low heart rate alerts.

Open heartbeat data

By default, Apple Watch monitors the heart rate of the "Heart Rate" app, tests, and breathing times. If you close your heartbeat data, you can turn it on again.

1. Exposed the "Settings" app on your Apple Watch.
2. Go to Privacy> Health.
3. Click "Heart Rate", then open "Heart Rate".

You can also open the Apple Watch app on your iPhone, tap on "My Watch", tap on "Privacy", and then open "Heart Rate".

Get high or low heart rate alerts

After idle action for at least 10 minutes, the Apple Watch will notify you if your heart rate remains above or below the selected threshold. You can turn on the heartbeat notification when you first open the Heart Rate app or at any time after that.

1. Exposed the "Settings" app on your Apple Watch and tap "Heart".
2. Tap "Heartbeat Notification" or "Low Heart Rate Notification", and set the heart rate limit.

You can also open the Apple Watch app on your iPhone, tap on "My Watch", and then tap on "Heart". click "High Heart Rate" or "Low Heart Rate" and set a boundary.

Receive unusual rhythm notifications (not available in all regions)

If your Apple Watch detects an arrhythmia that appears as atrial fibrillation (AFib), you will receive a notification.

1. Not built up the "Settings" app on your Apple Watch.
2. Tap "Heart" and open "Unusual Rhythm Notifications."

You can also open the Apple Watch app on your iPhone, tap on "My Watch", tap on "Heart", and then turn on "Irregular Rhythm".

Get cardio alerts

Apple Watch (with watchOS 7.2 or later) can measure your fitness level by checking your heart rate while walking or running outdoors and letting you know if your heart rate is low. Depending on your age and gender, your heart rate will fall into one of four categories: low, low, high, or high. If your exercise level is at a "low" level, then you will receive a notification on your Apple

Watch. If the price remains low, you will receive a notification every four months.

Note: This feature may not be accessible in all areas.

1. In the "Health" app on iPhone (using iOS 14.3 or later), tap "Browse", tap "Breath", and then tap "Aerobic Fitness".
2. Follow the on-screen instructions to turn on Cardio Fitness alerts.

You can also check the mirror standards of fitness and their range in the "Aerobics Fitness" section of the "Health" app. Click to show all levels of aerobic fitness.

Note: For best results, the back of the Apple Watch requires skin contact to detect the wrist, sensitive information, oxygen level (Apple Watch Series 6 only), and heart rate sensor. Wearing an Apple Watch properly (not too tight, too uncomfortable, and leaving skin space to breathe) can keep you comfortable and allow the sensor to function properly. For more information, see the Apple support Article "Wearing Apple Watch and Heart Rhythm." What it means and where it is on the Apple Watch.

Use the walkie-talkie on the Apple Watch

Walkie-Talkie is a fun and easy way to connect with other users with a compatible Apple Watch. Like using a real walkie-talkie, as long as you're ready for them to respond, you can press a button to speak, and then let go and listen. Walkie-Talkie requires both participants to have a Bluetooth connection via an iPhone, Wi-Fi, or mobile phone.

Note: Walkie-Talkie is not accessible in all constituencies.

Invite friends to use the walkie-talkie

1. Open the Walkie-Talkie app on the Apple Watch for the first time.
2. Scroll down the contact list and tap name to send the invitation.

After the contact has accepted the invitation, if both parties are available, you can start an intercom conversation.

To add a contact, click "Add Friend" on the "Intercom" screen and select a contact.

Have an intercom conversation

1. Open the Walkie-Talkie app on the Apple Watch.
2. Tap your friend's name.
3. Touch and hold the "Call" button, then speak.

When your friend is free, Walkie-Talkie will open on their Apple Watch and they will hear what you have to say.

To adjust the volume during a call, open the digital crown.

One-touch to speak

If you have difficulty pressing your finger on the "call" button, you can make a call with a single click.

1. Not built up the Settings app on your Apple Watch.
2. Click "Accessibility", then under "Intercom", open "Click to call".

After enabling this feature, click once to call, and then click again when the call is over.

You can also open the Apple Watch app on your iPhone, click "My Watch" and "Accessibility", then open "Tap to call" under "Intercom".

Delete contact

In the Walkie-Talkie app on the Apple Watch, swipe to the left of the contact and tap X.

Make yourself unavailable

1. Touch and hold at the bottom of the screen, then swipe up to open the control center.
2. Scroll up and tap the "Intercom" button.

Or, in the Walkie-Talkie app on the Apple Watch, scroll to the top of the screen, and close the Walkie-Talkie.

Turning on the theater mode will also prevent you from using the walkie-talkie.

Check the weather on the Apple Watch

Ask Siri. Say rather more like: "What's the prediction for Honolulu tomorrow?"

Check the weather conditions

- Check current temperature and day conditions: Open the "Weather" app on your Apple Watch. Click on a city, then click on Show to rotate hourly rainfall, conditions, or temperature forecasts.

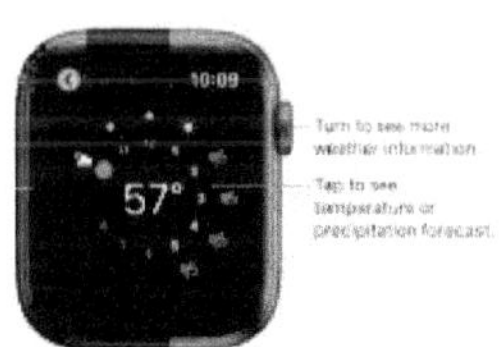

- View air quality, UV index, and airspeed information, and 10-day weather: click through the city, then descend.

Click <in the top left corner to return to the list of cities.

Note: Air quality readings are not available in all regions.

Add a city

1. Open the "Weather" app on your Apple Watch.
2. Scroll down to the list of cities, then click Add City.
3. Tap on "Dictation", "Smudge" or "Keyboard" and enter a city name.

Note: Graffiti is not available in all languages.

4. Click Finish, and then click a city name in the results list.

The Weather app on the iPhone shows the same cities in sequence as the Weather app has been added to the Apple Watch. For details on setting up an app for the iPhone, please refer to the iPhone User Guide.

Remove the city

1. Open the "Weather" app on your Apple Watch.
2. In the city list, swipe to the city you want to delete on the left, then tap X.

The city will be removed from Apple Watch and your iPhone.

Choose your default city

1. Open the "Settings" app on your Apple Watch.
2. Click "Weather", then "Default City", then select a city.

You can also open the Apple Watch app on your iPhone, tap on "My Watch", then go to "Weather"> "Default City".

If you add the weather to the dial, the location of the location will be shown in the dial.

Activity

Share your work from Apple Watch

Maintain strong habits by sharing tasks with family and friends, even coaches or trainers. You will receive notifications when your friends reach their goals, complete their applications and achieve success.

Add or remove friends

1. Open the Tasks program on your Apple Watch.
2. Swipe left, then not built up the digital crown to scroll to the end of the screen.
3. To add friends, click Invite friends, then click Friends

To delete a friend, click the friend you shared with you, then click "Delete."

After your friend accepts your invitation, you can see their activities and activities. If your friend does not accept the invitation, tap their name in the "Invitation" area on the "Share" screen, then click "Invite again."

To add friends, you can also open the "Fitness" app on your iPhone, click the "Share" tab, click the "Merge" button to add friends to the "To" field, or click on a suggested friend, then click send ".

Check the progress of friends

1. Open the "Tasks" program on your Apple Watch.
2. Swipe left, then open Digital Crown to scroll through your friend's list.
3. Tap a friend to view stats for the day.

Compete with your friends

Stay healthy and participate in this game. You can challenge your friends to participate in a contest where you earn points based on the percentage of closed job rings. With every percentage added to the ring every day, you'll get a point. The competition takes 7 days and can earn up to 600 points a day up to 4,200 points per week. The one with the highest score at the finale of the game wins. During the game, a warning will tell you whether you are in front of a competition or after a race school.

1. Open the "Tasks" program on your Apple Watch.
2. Swipe left, tap Friend, then tap "Run."
3. Click on the invitation and wait for your friend to accept it.

Or, if you get a "Work Sharing" notification (for example, your friend just closed the loop or doubled the moving target), you can scroll down and tap "Compete."

You can also open the "Fitness" app on your iPhone, click "Share", friend, and click "Compete with [your friend's name").

Change your friend's settings

You can easily adjust friend settings. Just exposed the Tasks app on your Apple Watch, swipe left, tap a friend, scroll down, and do any of the following:

- Mute notifications for friends: Tap Mute notifications.
- Hide your work from friends: Tap "Hide My Work".
- Delete friend: Click to delete friend.

Use the Apple Watch to track daily activities

The "work" app on Apple Watch monitors exercise throughout the day and encourages you to achieve your fitness goals. The app can track how often you stand, how often you exercise, and how long you exercise. Three colored circles summarize your progress. The goal is to complete each ring daily, reduce posture, exercise, and get more exercise.

The Fitness app on the iPhone will record your activity. If you have been following your workout for at least six months, it will show you daily data, including active calories, exercise time, stopping time, stopping time, walking distance, climbing a plane, and more. In the "Fitness" app on your iPhone, tap "Summary" and scroll to "Trends" to see how you compare to your average work.

Note: Apple Watch is not a medical device. For more info on the safe use of health apps, please refer to the Apple Watch Significant Information.

let's get started

When you set up your Apple Watch, you will be asked if you want to stop the "Activity" app. If you choose not to do so, you can do so when you first open the Jobs app.

1. Open the "Tasks" program on your Apple Watch.
2. Swipe left to read the "Move", "Exercise" and "Stand" instructions, then tap "Get Started".
3. Use Digital Crown to set your gender, age, height, weight, and wheelchair use.
4. Select the activity level and start submitting.

Check your progress

You can open the "Tasks" app on your Apple Watch at any time to understand your status. Active application shows three ringtones.

- The "moving" red ring indicates how many calories you have burned.
- The green "exercise" ring shows how many minutes you have spent exercising fast.
- The blue "stand" ring indicates the number of times you stand and move for at least one minute per hour during the day.

If you specify that you want to use a wheelchair, the green "standing" ring will be the "rolling ring" and indicate the number of times you have folded at least one minute per hour during the day.

Change the "digital crown" to view the full current scroll to view your drawings, complete steps, total distance, number of exercises, and the number of flights increased.

Skipping circles means you are more than your goal. Open the "digital crown" and tap "Summary of the week" to see what happened this week.

Change the goal

With watchOS 7, you can change each activity goal.

1. Open the "Tasks" program on your Apple Watch.
2. Open the "digital crown" to scroll to the bottom of the screen, then click "Change Goal".
3. Click the Delete button or the merge button for the correct adjustment, then click Next.

Every Monday, you will receive notifications about your success last week, and you can adjust your goals for next week. Your Apple Watch recommends objectives based on your previous performance.

View your work history

1. Open the Fitness app on your iPhone and tap Summary.
2. Tap the "Events" area, then tap the date.

Check out your styles

In the Fitness app for iPhone with iOS 14, the "Trend" area displays daily trend data, including activity calories, exercise time, stop time, stop time, walking distance, etc. Trends compare your work in the last 90 days with the last 365 days.

To view styles, follow these steps:

1. Open the "Fitness" app on your iPhone and tap "Summary".
2. Swipe up to see the trend.
3. To learn how to change the trend, click to see more.
4. To view a process history, click on it.

If the arrow of a certain target points upwards, it means that you are maintaining or improving your fitness level. If the arrow points to the ground, the average day eat 90 the index starts to decline. To help you reverse the trend, you will be given guidance, such as "walk a quarter of a meter more every day."

Look at your prize

You can use the Apple Watch to win prizes for your records, strokes, and big steps. To view all your prizes, including the "Activity Contest" prizes and the prizes you receive gradually, please follow the steps below:

1. Open the "Tasks" program on your Apple Watch.
2. Swipe left twice to view the "Awards" screen.
3. Scroll up to view your prizes. Tap a prize to learn more.

You can also open the "Fitness" app on your iPhone, tap the "Summary" tab, and swipe up to view "Awards" at the bottom of the screen.

For more information on the contest, see Competing with your friends, and for more details on support, see the Apple Support article Use the Apple Watch to earn event rewards.

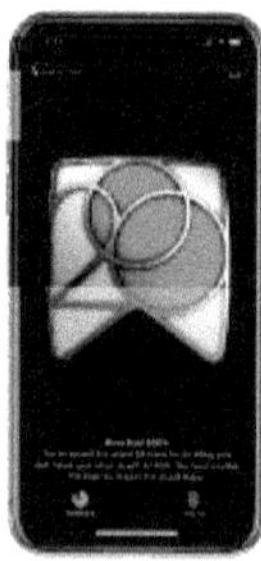

Remiendez control function

Reminders can help you achieve your goals. Your Apple Watch can let you know if you're on the road or following your sporting goals. To select the reminders and alarms you want to watch, follow these steps:

1. Open the Apple Watch app on your iPhone, then tap My Watch.
2. Click "Events" and set reminders.

Pause daily routines

To turn off event reminders, follow these steps:

1. Open the Apple Watch app on your iPhone, then tap My Watch.
2. Click "Tasks" and close "Daily Guidance".

HOME

Use the Apple Watch to control your home

The Home app provides a secure way to control and make HomeKit-enabled accessories, such as lamps, locks, thermostats, curtains, smart plugs, cameras, etc. With the Apple Watch, all gear sticks are on your wrist.

When you open the family app on your iPhone for the first time, the setup assistant will help you build a family. After that, you can define a room, add accessories that support HomeKit, and create a space. Attachments and scenes you add as favorites to the iPhone can be found on the Apple Watch. For details on setting up the home app on the iPhone, please refer to the iPhone User Guide.

Ask Siri. Say something like: "Turn off the office lights."

Add new accessories or groups to the home app

Use the Home app on iPhone to add accessories that support HomeKit or create a location. Your favorite accessories and scenes can be found on the Apple Watch.

1. To set an item as a favorite, go to the "Home" app on your iPhone and tap "Room".
2. Swipe left or right to find an accessory or scene, then touch and hold.
3. Click the "Settings" button, then open "Add to Favorites".

After adding a new attachment or group to your favorites, it will appear in the "Family" app on the Apple Watch.

Manage home accessories and scenes

1. Open the family app on Apple Watch.
2. Click the More Attach button, then adjust settings.
3. Swipe left to see more options.
4. To return to the attachment list, click Done.

To control the location, open the Home app on Apple Watch, and then tap a group to turn it on or off.

Look at other houses

Once you have set up multiple homes, you can choose which house to watch on the Apple Watch.

Open the home app on the Apple Watch, and do one of the following:

- When the Home screen is displayed, tap the Home screen.
- When the attachment screen is displayed, tap <, and then tap the house.

Send and receive intercom messages from Apple Watch

Using the home app on Apple Watch, you can send intercom messages to all internal members. You can also send intercom messages in the room or somewhere.

1. Open the home app on the Apple Watch, then tap the

intercom button.
2. Say something like "Who ate the last cookie?"
3. Click Finish.

Voice recordings will be sent to all HomePod speakers at home, as well as to iOS, iPadOS, and watchOS devices of all home members who send and receive intercom messages.

To send a message to the HomePod in a room or area, turn up your Apple Watch and say "Hello Siri, tell the office 'the movie has started'" or "Hello Siri, shout out, 'I'm going to the store.'"

Remotely access your smart home accessories from Apple Watch

If you live at home with Apple TV (third generation or later), HomePod, or iPad (iPadOS 13 or iOS 10 or later), you can remotely access HomeKit-enabled accessories from your iPhone and -Apple Watch paired. The Apple TV, HomePod, or iPad works as a home hub, allowing you to connect with accessories when you're not home.

Allow remote access

On the iPhone, go to "Settings"> "[your name]"> "Cloud" and open "Home". Be sure to sign in with the same Apple ID on all devices.

If you have an Apple TV and sign in with the same Apple ID as your iPhone, it will be paired automatically. To set up an iPad to allow remote access, please refer to the "Home" chapter of the "iPad User Guide".

Maps

Find a place and explore it with the Apple Watch

Your Apple Watch has a "map" app for exploring your surroundings and getting directions.

Ask Siri. Say this:

- "Where am I?"
- "Get coffee near me."

Warning: For important information about avoiding potential interference, see the Important Apple Watch Important Information.

Search the map

1. Not built up the Maps app on your Apple Watch.
2. Tap Search, then specify or find what you are looking for.

Note: Graffiti is not available in all languages.

Find nearby services

1. Exposed the Maps app on your Apple Watch.
2. Click "Search," and under "Near", click the category, such as "Food Delivery" or "Charge Channel."
3. Tap the result, then open Digital Crown to browse the information.
4. Click <in the top left corner to return to the results list.

Note: Not all regions offer close recommendations.

View guides for attractions and services nearby

1. Open the Maps app on your iPhone and do the following:
   - Tap the cover page that appears under "Editor's Editor."
   - Click "View All", then select the option at the top of the "All Guides" card, and click the cover.
   - Swipe down, select a printer, and then click the cover.
2. Click Save guide.

3. Open the "Maps" app on your Apple Watch.
4. Scroll down, select a publisher, and then click Guide.

For details on setting up and saving a guide in Maps, please refer to the iPhone User Guide.

View and search your current location and surroundings

1. Not built up the Maps app on your Apple Watch.
2. Click a location.
3. To search for your location, click the "More" button, then click "Search here."

Tap a transit map to see nearby travel options.

In the Apple Watch SE, Apple Watch Series 5, and Apple Watch Series 6, the blue tracker on the map shows the direction your watch is facing.

Pan and zoom

- Assemble the map: Drag with one finger.
- Zoom in or zoom out the map: Rotate the digital crown.

You can also double-tap the map to zoom in on location.

- Return to the current location: Click the "Location" button at the bottom left.

Find out about the location of the marker or marker

1. Tap the placemark on the map.
2. Open the digital crown to scroll details.
3. Click <Back to map in the top left corner.

Tip: To call a location, click the phone number in the location information. To switch to iPhone, open the app switch. (For iPhone with Face ID, swipe up from the bottom edge and pause;

for iPhone with the home button, double-click the Home button.) Tap the button at the bottom of the screen to turn on "Phone."

Place, move and remove map anchors

- Put down the pin: Touch and hold the map where you want to raise the pin, wait for the pin to drop, and then release.
- Move pushpin: Put a new pushpin in a new position
- Remove pushpin: Tap to view address details, rotate the digital crown to scroll, and then tap Remove marker.

Tip: To find the nearest address of any place on the map, place a PIN in the area, and then tap the PIN to view address details.

View the contact's address on the map

1. Not built up the Maps app on your Apple Watch.
2. Click Search, and then click the Contact button.
3. Open the number crown to scroll, then tap the address.
4. Scroll down and tap the map.

Get instructions on the Apple Watch

Ask Siri. Say this:

- "Road to the nearest garage?"
- "Home instructions"
- "How far is it from the airport?"

Get directions

1. Exposed the Maps app on your Apple Watch.
2. Rotate the digital crown to scroll to "Favorites", "Guide"

and "Recent".

3. Tap input for information on travel, driving, public transportation, and bike paths.

Note: Not all shipping methods are available everywhere.

4. Tap mode to view suggested routes, then tap route to start the trip and view its entire view (including turns, the distance between turns, and street names).

Tip: If you select "Bicycling", you will see a full view of the transition height. Tap the "More" button to learn the type of road you're going to take (whether it has bike lanes, sidewalks or highways, or requires you to lower your bike and walk).

After leaving the first stop, Apple Watch will use sounds and taps to let you know when you turn it on. Low key and high key (marking, ck) mean right turn at the intersection of the approximate road; up and down (limit, limit) means to turn left. Not sure where to go? When you get to the last stop and when you arrive, you will feel a shock.

Check the top left corner to see your estimated arrival time.

To close a route before reaching your destination, tap <left at the top of the screen, then tap Finish.

Select unlock warning

If you use a turn-by-turn route, the Apple Watch will remind you when you need to make the next turn. To select the turnaround warning you want to receive, follow these steps:

1. Open the Apple Watch app on your iPhone.
2. Tap my watch, then tap the map.
3. Turn on the alerts you want to drive — driving, driving with CarPlay, walking, and cycling.

Note: Location services must be turned on for turn-by-turn operations. On Apple Watch, go to "Settings"> "Privacy"> "Location Services" to turn location services on or off.

Get directions to a global map or map

1. Open the "Maps" app on your Apple Watch.
2. Tap "Location," then tap the destination or pin map.
3. Scroll to location information until you see "Directions", then choose hiking, driving, public transportation, or bike directions.
4. When you are ready to leave, tap the route and follow the instructions.

Ask Siri. Say this: "How long will it take me to go home?"

Quickly return to the "map" on the clock face

Once you get the route instructions, you can switch to the clock face. To quickly return to the map, tap the status bar icon at the top of the screen.

View transit

With the route shown in the Map app, you can select various options before you start.

- Choose an alternative: When another option appears, tap one.
- Switch to driving route, hiking, transport, or cycling: tap hiking, driving, transporting, or cycling.
- Avoid toll booths or highways: For driving route indicators, tap> and open the option.
- Avoid steep hills or busy roads: For a bike path indicator, tap> and open the option.
- Select your preferred public transportation: For the indicated bus route, tap> and select your preferred public transport mode, such as bus, subway, and subway, passenger train, and boat.

Phone

Make emergency calls on the Apple Watch

In case of an emergency, please use your Apple Watch for immediate assistance.

Emergency call

Do any of the subsequent:

- Press and grip the sidebar until a slide appears, then drag the "Emergency SOS" slider to the right.

Apple Watch will call emergency services in your zone, such as 911. (In some cases, you may need to press the keyboard number keys to complete the call.) After the call is completed, Apple Watch will remind the emergency contact to make a call and send it to your location (if available).

- Press and hold the side button until the Apple Watch beeps and the countdown starts. At the end of the count, the Apple Watch will call emergency services. The Apple Watch will sound even in silent mode, so if you don't want to make noise in an emergency, use the "Emergency SOS" slider to make emergency calls instead of counting down.

If you do not want your Apple Watch to automatically start an emergency calculation when you press and hold the side-bar, please turn off "Auto Dial". Open the "Settings" app on Apple Watch, click on "SOS", then click on "Save Button", then turn off "Save Button". (Or open the Apple Watch app on your iPhone, tap My Watch, tap Emergency SOS, then turn off the Grip Side Button.) You can still use the "Emergency SOS" slider to do so. emergency calls.

If fall detection work is allowed, and it stops about one minute after the Apple Watch has received a serious fall, it will automatically call emergency services. See Manage fall discovery on Apple Watch.

You can use Apple Watch Series 5 (GPS + cellular phone), Apple Watch SE (GPS + cellular phone), or Apple Watch Series 6 (GPS + cell phone) to make emergency calls in most places, as long as the mobile phone services are available. If your Apple Watch does not work, is not compatible with a particular mobile network, or is unable to operate on a specific mobile network, some mobile networks may not accept emergency calls from Apple Watch Series 5, Apple Watch SE, or Apple Watch Series 6.., Or not set for mobile phone service.

Share your medical ID and emergency services

1. Not built up the Apple Watch app on your iPhone.
2. Tap on My Clock and go to Health Medical ID.
3. Click Edit and then open Share during emergency calls.

To create your medical ID, see Create an emergency medical ID.

Cancel emergency call

If you accidentally start an emergency call, please click the "End call" button, then click "End Call" to cancel.

Enter an emergency contact

1. Open the "Health" app on your iPhone.
2. Click on your profile picture, click on "Medical ID", then click on "Edit".
3. Click "Add an emergency contact" and then click "Done" to save your changes.

Answer calls on Apple Watch

Warning: For important information about avoiding potential interference, see the Important Apple Watch Important Information.

answer the phone

When you hear or hear a call notification, lift your wrist to see who is in the call.

- Send call to voicemail: Click the red reject button in the incoming call notification.
- Response to Apple Watch: Tap the "Answer" button to use the built-in microphone and speaker or Bluetooth device paired with the Apple Watch to make calls.
- Use iPhone to reply or send messages: Tap the "More" button, then tap the option. When you click "Reply" on the iPhone, the call will be answered and the caller will hear the repeated sound until you answer it on the paired iPhone.

If you can't find your iPhone, touch and hold the bottom of the screen, swipe up, and then tap the Ping Phone button on your Apple Watch.

On the phone

If you do not use FaceTime audio during a call, you can switch the phone to an iPhone, adjust the volume of calls, use the keypad to enter numbers and switch the phone to another audio device.

- Switch phone from Apple Watch to iPhone: When dialing the Apple Watch, turn on the iPhone, and tap the green button or the green bar at the top of the screen.

You can immediately mute incoming calls you press and hold the palm of your hand on the display screen for three seconds. Just make sure "Set Mute to mute" is turned on - open the "Settings" app on your Apple Watch, click on "Sounds and Haptics", and then open "Set Mute to mute".

- Adjust call volume: Change digital crown. Tap the "Mute" button to mute the end of the call (for example, when you listen to a conference call).
- Enter some numbers during the call: click the button above, click the keyboard, and then click the numbers.
- Switch call to an audio device: Tap the "More" button, then select the device.

During a FaceTime audio call, you can adjust the volume, mute the phone by pressing the mute button, or pressing the volume up key, and selecting your audio destination.

Listen to voicemail

When the caller leaves the voicemail, you will receive a notification - click the "Play" button on the notification to listen. To listen to voicemail later, open the "Phone" app on your Apple Watch and tap "Voice Mail."

In the voice mail screen, you can select the following:

- Adjust the volume with Digital Crown
- Start and stop playing
- Jump forwards or backward for five seconds
- call back
- Delete voicemail

Use dual SIM card with Apple Watch mobile model

If you have set many cellular strategies for an iPhone with Dual SIM, you can add multiple lines to the Apple Watch with mobile phones, and select the line used when the clock is connected to a mobile network.

Note: Each iPhone mobile package must be supplied with a supported carrier and must support Apple Watch phones.

Set up multiple operator settings

When you set your watch for the first time, you can add a schedule. You can set up a second version of the Apple Watch app later in the following steps:

1. Not built up the Apple Watch app on your iPhone.
2. Tap on my watch, then tap on the phone.
3. Click Set Up Cellular or Add New Plan, and follow the steps to select the program you want to install on

Apple Watch.

You can add multiple lines to the Apple Watch, but the Apple Watch can only connect to one line at a time.

Switch between programs

1. Exposed the Settings app on your Apple Watch.
2. Tap "Mobile" and select the application you want to use with your watch.

You can also open the Apple Watch app on your iPhone, tap on "My Watch", and then tap on "Cellular Phone". Your schedule should change automatically. If there is no switch, click the application you want to use.

How the Apple Watch answers call when using multiple mobile devices

- When the Apple Watch is connected to the iPhone: You can receive calls from two lines. The badge will be displayed on your watch to tell you which cell phone line the notification received, for example, home H and W for activity. When you answer a call, your watch will automatically answer from the line where the call was received.
- When the Apple Watch is connected to a cell phone and the iPhone is not nearby: You will answer a call from a selected line in the Apple Watch app. When you answer a call, the clock will automatically dial from the selected line in the Apple Watch app.

Note: If the selected line in the Apple Watch app is not available when you try to make a call, the clock will ask you if you want to answer from another installed line.

How the Apple Watch receives messages when using multiple applications

- When the Apple Watch is connected to the iPhone: You can receive messages from two programs. When you reply to a message, your watch will automatically reply from the queue where the message was received.

- When the Apple Watch is connected to a cell phone and not on the iPhone: You can receive SMS messages from the app. When you reply to an SMS message, Apple Watch will automatically send an SMS from the line where the message was received.
- When Apple Watch is connected to a mobile network or Wi-Fi and the iPhone is turned off: As long as the Apple Watch has an active data connection over Wi-Fi or mobile network, it can send and receive iMessage messages.

Make calls on Apple Watch

Ask Siri. Say this:

- "Phone Limit"
- "Call 555 555 2949"
- "Call Pete FaceTime Audio"

Call

1. Not built up the phone app on your Apple Watch.
2. Tap Contacts, then open the digital crown to scroll.
3. click the dealings you want to call, then click the phone button.
4. click FaceTime Audio to start a FaceTime audio call, or tap a phone number.
5. During a call, turn on Digital Crown to adjust the volume.

Tip: To call someone you've recently spoken to, tap "Recent" and then tap the contact. To call your favorite person in the "Phone" iPhone app, tap "Favorites" and then tap the contact.

Enter the phone number on the Apple Watch

1. Exposed the phone app on your Apple Watch.
2. Tap the keyboard, enter the number, and then tap the

call button.

You can also use the keypad to enter additional numbers during a call. Just click the "More" button and then the "Keyboard" button.

Make calls over Wi-Fi

If your mobile operator provides a Wi-Fi call, even if your paired iPhone is missing or turned off, you can use Apple Watch to make and receive calls over Wi-Fi instead of a mobile network. Your Apple Watch needs to be within the Wi-Fi network your iPhone was previously connected to.

To see if your carrier offers you Wi-Fi hits, check out the Apple support article Use Wi-Fi hits to make calls and enable Wi-Fi hits on your iPhone.

1. On your iPhone, go to "Settings"> "Phone", tap "Wi-Fi Calls", then turn on "Wi-Fi Calls" and "Add Wi-Fi Calls from Other Devices" to this iPhone at the same time.
2. Open the "phone" app on your Apple Watch.
3. Select a contact and click the "Call" button.
4. Choose your phone number or FaceTime address and drive it.

Note: You can make emergency calls over Wi-Fi, but if possible, please use your iPhone via cellular connection to keep your location information accurate. Make sure your emergency address is up to date on your iPhone, go to Settings, Phone, Wi-Fi hitting and click Update emergency address". If paramedics do not find you, they will go to your emergency address.

View phone details in Apple Watch

When making a call on your iPhone, you can view the phone details in the "Phone" app on your Apple Watch. You can also turn off the phone with an Apple Watch (for example, when using earphones or headphones).

Apple Watch Series 6 tips and tricks

The new Apple Watch Series 6 has some great improvements based on the Apple Watch Series 4 and Series 5. Not only is it fast, but smartwatches can now track your blood oxygen levels, sleep, and more. If you have recently purchased the new Apple Watch Series 6, please check out the tips and tricks about it, which will help you to make full use of it and get all its features.

Some of the improvements and changes Apple made in the Apple Watch Series 6 are obvious, while others are less obvious. Below, we've collected some useful tips and tricks, and features highlighted by the Apple Watch Series 6, otherwise, you won't miss out on these features.

Use a stock charger

Unlike previous models of the Apple Watch, the Apple Watch Series 6 comes with faster charging support. This allows the wearable device to be fully charged at 0-50% of power in just 40 minutes, while the full charge takes about 1.5 hours. However, to enjoy full charging speed on the Apple Watch, it is important to use a separate charger with a 10W power adapter for the device. This is important because external wireless chargers on the market can only charge the Apple Watch with a maximum speed of 2.5W.

Constantly improved display

Like the previous Apple Watch Series 4 and Series 5, the Apple Watch Series 6 also has regular support. The good news is that Apple has improved its use of Always Display, increasing its brightness by 2.5 times. This means that regularly displayed content will be easier to read than before, especially when traveling.

it is not. Apple has also upgraded the display mode regularly and now allows users to directly access the notification center, control center and tap the difficulty without triggering the display of the wearable device.

Always-in altimeter

Apple uses the new altimeter in the Apple Watch Series 6, which provides real-time data. This is possible because the company is using an energy-efficient altimeter, which can also retrieve data from GPS and Wi-Fi networks. This not only makes the new altimeter more accurate - it can detect changes with just one foot, but it also has higher operating efficiency. Thanks to this upgrade, you can get real-time data from an altimeter, as a complex diagram, or as an exercise indicator in the Apple Watch Series 6.

Improve your communication skills with Siri

Siri may not be as smart as Google Assistant or Alexa, but you can still use it to set reminders and complete other tasks easily. Apple also makes calls with Siri much easier. Whenever you need to start an assistant, just raise your wrist and say "Hello Siri", and start talking to the assistant. This minimizes conflict when talking to a visual assistant and improves its usability.

Pass the notifications silently to the Apple Watch

You can choose to deliver notifications from other apps directly to the Notification Center. This will not remind you when you receive a new notification. This setting will also be synced with the iPhone. This is significant if you receive a lot of notices every day. Not all notices are important, and your Apple Watch does not require a buzz.

The next time you want to send a notification silently, swipe the notification to the left of the Apple Watch, then tap the menu button. Then select the "Quiet Send" option. If you want to change your mind, you can add "Significant Delivery" later.

Use Apple Watch as a remote control for the camera

Open the "Camera" app on Apple Watch and it will instantly launch the "Camera" on iPhone. After that, you can tap the shoot button on the Apple Watch to take a picture or use the timer.

Use Theater Mode

Sometimes, you don't want your Apple Watch to light up every time you move your hand or get a call or a notification. Swipe up to access the control center, then tap the theater mode icon to enable it. Sure, most of us have never been to a movie for months, but this is a very useful mode, whether you are attending a very important meeting or a video call.

Ring your iPhone

Your iPhone is in silent mode, can't find where it was finally stored? You can catch it with your Apple Watch. Open the "Control Center" in the Apple Watch Series 6, then click the "iPhone" button to hold it. This way, even in silent mode, your iPhone will make a sound so you can easily find it.

Cover the Apple Watch to mute it

When the Apple Watch blows, makes noise, or lights up at bad times, just cover it with the palm of your hand to mute the sound, touch response or just turn off the screen.

Hide monitoring application

Even if you have enabled the option to sync all available viewing apps, you can choose to hide or disable any Watch apps. Open the "Monitoring" app, find the problematic program, and turn off the "Show application on Apple Watch" option.

Getting hand washing

In the current situation, it is important to wash your hands regularly. The Apple Watch can help you with this, as it can often remind you to wash your hands when you return home.

The handwashing job will ask you to wash your hands for 20 seconds. If you stop washing your hands before that, the clock will give you a relevant response to encourage you to continue washing your hands. And it's not easy to trick this feature, because Apple uses a microphone to listen to tap water and another high-quality algorithm to decide whether to wash your hands.

Read: How to use the hand-washing detection function on the Apple Watch

Use Siri to translate languages

You no longer need to use an iPhone to quickly translate languages, like using Siri on an Apple Watch.

You can quickly start Siri and request a language change. Select the Apple Watch microphone to display words and phrases, and let Siri translate them into other languages (from a set of supported languages).

To date, Siri on Apple Watch supports 10 languages, including Spanish, English, Japanese, Arabic, Chinese, and Russian.

Use Siri Shortcuts

Apple has introduced Siri Shortcuts to watchOS 7, so you can now use Siri Shortcuts directly to Apple Watch. You can also add

Siri shortcut actions as a sophisticated clock face to quickly remove them from your wrist.

Use Siri to announce the news

In some cases, this may be easier. With watchOS 7 and Apple Watch Series 6, where second-generation AirPods and some Beats headphones are connected to the iPhone, you can ask Siri to read the messages. Just open the control center and use the declare message button to use this function.

Third-party viewing strips

It is very easy to replace the Apple Watch Series 6. belt If you are unsure, you can also use a third-party belt. This is because Apple uses the same lock method as standard watches, so you can use an unrestricted belt in the selection.

Measure your blood oxygen level

Apple introduces a new blood-monitoring system in the Apple Watch Series 6. There is also a new "blood oxygen" system that can be used to measure your oxygen supply. However, before using a blood oxygen sensor, you should first stop it. To do this, open the "Health" app on your iPhone, and you'll automatically find information here to set up a blood oxygen app. If not, go to the Browse tab, then go to Respiration> Spo2> Set SpO2. After that, you can use the Apple Watch to open the "Blood Oxygen" app to measure blood oxygen levels.

Whenever you take a measure, make sure the watch fits snugly on your wrist. Please note that the application of blood oxygen in the Apple Watch Series 6 is currently only available in certain regions.

Customize your eligibility goals

With watchOS 7, Apple finally allows users to customize their waiting time and workout time. So, if you want to set your fitness goals more than other goals, you can set yourself time limits for standing and minutes for exercise.

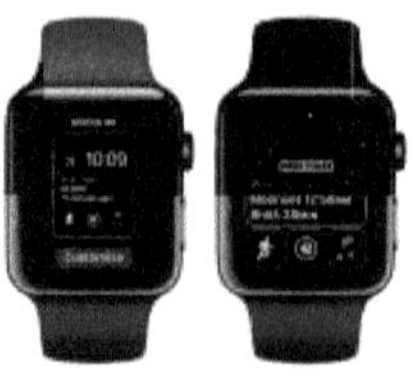

Increasing text size

If you have a larger version of the Apple Watch with 44mm, you can pay less to increase the text size. To do this, go to Settings Brightness and text size".

Use Digital Crown to control the volume

If you're on the "Play Now" screen of any app, just use the digital crown to control the volume. You can do this without looking at or activating the screen.

Answer calls to iPhone from Apple Watch

When your iPhone is close, you can answer calls on your Apple Watch. However, it is better not to talk too long. After receiving the call, scroll up to find the "answer" button on the iPhone. You can also transfer ongoing calls to the iPhone this way.

Share the face of the clock

Do you like the beautiful clock face on your friend's Apple Watch? You can now share your face clock via SMS, email, or online posting links. You can also get new face clocks from the App Store or the Internet. Your friends can now share the layout, and you can emulate architecture fixes on Apple Watch.

Remove the switch from the control center

Now you can finally remove the switch from the Apple Watch control center. You will view an Edit button in the control center. Click on it, and it will allow you to remove unwanted toggles from the control center.

www.ingramcontent.com/pod-product-compliance
Ingram Content Group UK Ltd.
Pitfield, Milton Keynes, MK11 3LW, UK
UKHW022024190726
13853UKWH00005B/2105

9 798515 680527